COMPASS OF THE DYING

BOOKS BY
Laurence Lieberman

POETRY

CRITICISM

Compass of the Dying

POEMS BY
Laurence Lieberman

The University of Arkansas Press
Fayetteville   1998

02   01   00   99   98   5   4   3   2   1

Designed by Alice Gail Carter

☻ The paper used in this publication meets the mini-
mum requirements of the American National Standard
for Permanence of Paper for Printed Library Materials
Z39.48-1984.

Library of Congress Cataloging-in-Publication Data

Lieberman, Laurence.
    Compass of the dying : poems /
by Laurence Lieberman.
        p.   cm.
        ISBN 1-55728-509-8 (cloth : alk. paper). —
    ISBN 1-55728-510-1 (pbk. : alk. paper)
        I. Title
    PS3562.I43C6   1998   97-37473
                                      CIP

*for Jesse Asher
my grandson*

Acknowledgments

I wish to thank the editors of the following magazines, in which these poems first appeared:

American Poetry Review: "Wide Skull, Puffy Jowls,"
"Spine," "The Origin of Stars"

Arkansas Review: "The Chinese Gambling House,"
"Massikuriman: The River Demons"

Beloit Poetry Journal: "Urn Burial"

Boulevard: "Dry River Crossing," "Compass of the
Dying," "A Gift of Tusks"

The Caribbean Writer: "Work Chants at an Abandoned
Gold Mill"

The Carrell: "Ladyknife"

The Chariton Review: "The Morning Star, Extinguished,"
"Notes from the Synagogue Museum"

Denver Quarterly: "Farewell to the Lost Music Scores"

The Hudson Review: "Embracing the Sisserou Parrot,"
"Romp of the Cave Healer"

The Journal of Caribbean Literatures: "Ballad of the Star
Hijackers"

Kenyon Review: "The Marriage Furies," "Three Years
after the Four Days' War," "Hosting an Idol"

The Nation: "Undying Loyalty"

River City: "The Iguana Hunter's Floating Gait"

Sewanee Review: "Thirst"

The Southern Review: "By the Light of One Star,"
"Lament for the Lady Felons"

Tar River Poetry: "The Legend of Rode Pan Well,"
"Shaggy Mane Lord"

"Lament for the Lady Felons" was reprinted in *The World's Best Poetry, 1997,* edited by Harvey Roth.

Special thanks to the Center for Advanced Study and the Program for the Study of Cultural Values and Ethics at University of Illinois for creative writing fellowships, which supported the completion of this book.

Contents

I.

Undying Loyalty

We approach a tall pier,
hitch up, and disembark at Fort Island. Chat with local Indians
selling their wares. Then make our way, trudging
through sodden marsh, to the old Dutch Catholic Church—kept up
in the bleak style of 1767,
within view of the ruins
of stronghold
Fort Zeelandia, at the tiny isle's far end.
The bare church comprises
but two rooms:
a front chamber for *stand-up* prayer meetings
(benches and pews, if any
there were, long
since removed), and a rear
sanctuary: the chapel's oddly punitive tone evoked by an oblong
grave-setting in midfloor, some former churchman
buried therein, topped by shallow gravestone, forbidding skull
& crossbones embossed above.

This church, we learn,
was ruled by the Fort, the rear room doing double duty as lockup
and torture annex, complete with high-wall recess
or alcove that held—if we can believe it—an indoors guillotine.
The Dutch colonial *top brass,*
that moneyed elite, lorded it
over all churchmen.
Suspects were questioned here, the accused
indicted and tried on the spot,
then dispatched
to the adjunct crawl space, a homemade jail . . .
We take a quick sloshy hike
to the fort ruins,

some few walls left standing,
high thick crossbeams of *greenheart wood* still intact—no cracks
or warp anyplace, over these hundreds of years.
Out back, we find a row of obscure graves, half-hidden by a semi-
circular brick enclosure.

Here, in extra-deep
fake tombs, family treasures of the ruling patrons were buried,
the bank vaults disguised as crypts. Each master
had bid his most faithful slave to dig a deep pit, then to lower
the lavish oaken casket
(jampacked with jewels, gold
& silver ingots,
all precious brooches, goblets, antiques)
into fresh-dug hole. Next,
without prior
briefing, each slave was coerced to twist
a prize dagger round about
in his own innards,
his life's blood pouring forth
upon the coffin top. Buried promptly, his disemboweled carcass
lay sprawled over valuables entrusted to his care.
Dead, he'd never divulge the true contents of the grave, his loyal
spirit presiding evermore . . .

A Gift of Tusks

(Essequibo River, Guyana)

Big scare today, in coastal Saxicali
Village. Two young boys
were gathering sticks, tinder
for kindling fires
in home-
hearth wood stoves,
no more than one bush-mile inland
from shoreline town limits
(that one circle
of homes

      & stores)
when, without
provocation or warning,
a pack of wild hogs, tusks lowered,
charged them! The boys,
both fleet
of foot, scampered
to nearest trees & scaled a trunk
before they were hit.
Thereupon, the boars circled & howled.

Pounded bark with their upraised tusks,
at short intervals—
momentary flare-ups. Then milled
about, stalking
the human
prey, as if never
to leave . . . Wild hogs often travel
in pairs, sneak side-by-side
into the village
by night

to ransack
garbage, but rarely
are seen in larger packs
near town (great hordes of forty
or fifty may be
spotted,
sometimes, by lucky
hunting parties—deep in Guyana's
interior) . . . Today,
word drifted back of boys' entrapment

in treetop, their two dogs limping home,
one badly wounded
by tusk in groin—the giveaway.
On shortest notice,
small troops
of off-duty crack
fishermen assemble near the woods,
armed with bows & arrows,
no few machetes,
hatchets.

Whole town
astir, the elders
are hopeful a major routing
of boars may ensue, thus to assuage
shortage of hog meat
for months
to come . . . *Yaiee, Yaiee!*
As we chat, we hear distant cries
like monkey gibbers.
But nearer, those voices—reverberant

and shrill—diverge into dual choruses:
pursuers & pursued,
the men grunting low chesty roars
of attack, *Yaiee*,
as they

let fly arrows
from the long bows, while the pigs,
stampeding, hotly driven
toward shore, shriek
& trumpet

raw terror.
The fierce hairy swine,
leaping from widespread gaps
in the forest, converge as they race
toward coastline
and open
water, many hitting
the low weedy surf at once, cluster
by manic cluster;
curly tails and purplish snouts erupting

everywhere, while they swim, lumberingly,
those bobbing rotund
muskmelon-shaped butts crowded upon
each other. Again
and again,
they collide
in frenzy of escape . . . Still armed
with varieties of wood-
handled hardware,
men pile

hurriedly
into sleek long-nosed
fish boats, loosely tethered
to the dock. One captain amicably taps
my shoulder. *You come,*
come learn
the hunt, he says,
and draws me after him . . . I'm seated
low in cigar-shaped
long boat. The skipper gives me a nominal

job paying out ropes from two tight-wound
                        reels on either side
        of the bow. Four men to my rear
                    brandish weapons
                            overhead,
                and at the ready.
    Our small motor quickly revs up
        high speeds, fast shrinking
                the hog pack's lead,
                    cumbersome

                        swimmers all,
                        wallowing & jerking
                        from side to side. Now we zoom in
                        upon a frantic hog trio, splintered off
                        from that snorting herd
                        huddled
                        stupidly together
                        as they swim. Two men in the stern
                        take up positions,
                        the boat swung about to put them directly

over the runaway threesome, both lightning-
            quick arms coming down
        before I've seen paired shoulders
                    upswept & angled
                            for strikes.
                One gaunt man wields
    a small short-handled ax, his zippy
        up-and-down motion hacking
                    off a rear hunk
                        of boar's

                        head or neck
                        (who can tell which
                        is which, where they conjoin
                        long neck with eyes twirls into snout,
                        all one jointless

rubbery
forepart); his seat
mate swings a long cutlass, from left
to right and back.
Two hogs spurt blood from flanks, the blade

still flying so fast in either direction
it's a wild blur.
A severed hind leg leaps skyward.
I see the pointy
two-toed
hoof whirling
over the boat's prow, spirals of gut
uncoiling on the calm river's
face. Two more pigs
twist away

from droves.
Single quick ax blows
to the head, skull riveners,
quiet both. Soon I'm wheeling out ropes
from both spools, feeding
slack loops
to the men port side
and aft, who quickly snap the tossed
cords into lassoes,
flinging them over heads of wounded swine.

They fasten each noosed deadweight of hairy
blubber to boat gunnel
rails, while I hop this way & that,
shifting my flabby mass
to balance
strong drags to one side—
nearly upending us twice when heftiest
pigs were tied in place, feet
upswung in air,
snorting

& gargling
against the tight noose.
Finally, swamping much water
and laden with hog carcass tugging
at all sides, boats churn,
haltingly,
to shore, while a lineup
of women—carrying buckets & meat
cleavers—goes plunging
into the shallows to greet incoming crews.

They start swinging & hacking long before
the boats near dockside,
all pails quickly filled with choice
hog parts . . . Our skipper
twists off
two prime curved tusks,
stringing them on short leather lanyard
around my neck: two-pronged pendant,
my false-ivory
keepsake.

Massikuriman: The River Demons

1.

Val Rempadoo, native
Guyanese who left his riverine homeland at age nine
and resettled with his family
in Trinidad, whips up
a nostalgia high . . .
This week's his first return visit since he migrated
Upislands: due North
twenty years back. Tall, lean and lithe as a jaguar,
wriggling this way
and that, Val stretches long legs below my seat—
sunk low on bench slats directly
to my rear. And I must do

a quick shuffle of limbs, to keep from trampling upon
his far-flung feet as he mutters
that constant running fact sheet of Guyana
lore, myth and history blent.
Trained botanist,

he explores rare trees
and flowers in the bush—FINDINGS: three new species
of wild jungle orchid, promptly
named and domesticated,
are ascribed to Val's
lucky hunts. His blest nursery in Port-of-Spain,
a prodigal export
business, sends him abroad for frequent long sojourns
in Ireland, Wales,
and *The Continent,* to peddle his rare mosses, vines,
shrubs, and flowering trees. He finds
me avid for fact. Ah yes,

I tap right into his flow . . . Cruising at a smart clip,
we hit a magical blank calm
in the river. Not a stir, or least rumpling
of surface, breaks the mirror's
stark purity.

There's no gradient,
no gradient here, Val explains. *So the mild currents*
balance each other out—neutralize.
But the helmsman lunges,
without warning. Our boat
swoops left, then right, zigzags: some dips so sharp
he swamps our gunnels
(we take turns bailing out puddles at our feet, passing
the scoop basin
to & fro) . . . *Why must we swerve, wildly, in placid waters,*
I ask Val? *To dodge savage arms*
of coral reefs, near-hidden

below the sheen of pool face, he says. *You can't depend*
on sight in these mucky waters,
most treacherous coral wings rarely visible
from above. Our driver knows
every coral

ramrod—hull mauler
or keel buckler—that lurks below: yes, he must swerve
most fitfully in waters that appear
most tame. We round a bend
near the peninsula—
abrupt shift in current swings us about by some ninety
degrees, and we skirt
a wicked rapids, many rocky nubs and wedges peeking
through white water
foams. This maze of stone claws, half-visible/half-
submerged, is greedy to dismember
and swallow unwary boaters.

The whole passage, abutting on steep falls, is a *Widow*
Maker. Dozens of lost travelers,
     per year, just vanish from river shallows
or depths, alike. So few bodies
wash ashore,

                    Lord only knows what
          becomes of them down there. And when small children
                         drown, a great furor is babbled
                    around the wharves and boat
                              moorings for a spell,
but soon forgotten . . . *MASSIKURIMAN, he's the culprit,*
                    Val groans, pointing
          at a tangle of forked rock arms. *Who, I ask? Is he some*
                         negligent river
               marshall, or Coast Guard boss, to blame for the failed
               safety record—that big up-tick
                              in drownings, year after year? . . .

          2.

Massikuriman. The River Demon. He's always down there,
     hiding among the rocks, his wispy
     knotted hair locks disguised as seaweeds
or rubbery clinging vines.
Those tubers

                    attached to rock side
          by suckers could be his fingers, or claws. We think
                         we see rows of barnacles, leeches,
                    but they're all his cleverly
                              disguised black talons.
He waits and waits. No limits to his staying power,
                    appetites ravenous,
     he prefers youth, lads and lasses in the prime of life—
                              who know they'll live
          forever. Nothing can hurt them. They shoot the rapids
               in flimsy shells, little dugout
                              boat tubs. It is he who sucks

them under. They defy his threats, laugh in the teeth
of his briny scowls. And he takes
their insults *personal,* his hunger for fresh
young hides whetted by revenge.
Thus, he thrives,

                              lives off young bloods.
            Your kind call him a myth, or mere fairy tale jester.
                              To the Church, he's a late fallen
                    angel, Satan's minion.
                                        But he's Essequibo
River's true demon. All river folk dread and lament
                    his terrible blows.
        It can't be helped. Massikuriman, the elusive, shies away
                                        from battle—he won't
            be defeated, though mild truce is possible. Take utmost
            care in passage, as does our skipper
                                        today. We travelers best guard

        our safety by respect, respect paid to his measureless
        powers. If tragedy strikes, we know
        the River Demon has reared his scabrous head,
taking swipes with horns disguised
as shark fins;

                              or he may strangle
            victims with his tail, masqueraded as a sea snake
                                    or moray eel. The monster takes
                    many forms, turns disseveral
                                        to better fool prey,
but all branches spring from—and return to—the one
                    hidden dark trunk . . .
        There are shore demons, too, riverbank fiends who hide
                                    in old rotted-tree
            hollows like elf owls, or lurk in river-bottom sludge
                    washed ashore, putrefying beach mucks.
                                    Many small children, last seen

playing on the riverside, seem to vanish—they go poof
in an eye blink. Never to return.
    Grownups, who supervised their play and let
their vigilance lapse one moment,
looking aside

                              for the brief space
    of a sigh, a sneeze, or two hiccups maybe, are left
                              holding children of spindrift,
                    the offspring of flotsam,
                                    sprigs of river weed
in their arms. O pound their foreheads and chests
                    with snail shells,
    or thrash their backs and shoulders with bamboo switch,
                              or prick their skins
        with painful needles daubed in stinging bitter potions
            though they shall—it's to no avail.
                              To no avail, the vast search

    parties, most able-bodied men of the village dredging
    the river floor through the night,
        next day and night, dragging up the bottom
debris and shifting through all
the old fish boat

                    spillage of rotted
    ropes and sails and rusted motor parts . . . O always,
                    the lost child *stays lost,* vanishes
            without a trace, disappears
                              without a cry or howl
for ears of the newly bereaved to snatch from the wind,
                    some pang of the ear
    or eye to enshrine the loss, the void left in space.
                    No mark, no sign,
        no voice palliates the gap, the fluttering vacancy.
            And we know beyond doubt, beyond help,
                    the *Pia man* has snapped them up,

that lordly enticer who lures our young pale children
with the beautiful shapely drooped
lobes of his ears. We know he beckons them
with those graceful ear loops
stretched and grooved

         by his weighty stone
pendants, floppy ear parts dangled below his jawbone,
         or below his first and second ribs
perhaps. O how he jiggles
         and puckers and wags
those wonderful fleshly appurtenances, as he beckons
         the children to come
ride, come ride, play horsey on his neck and shoulders,
         slipping their bare
or sandaled feet through those rubber-doll elastic
         stirrups of his low-slung pouchy ears.
         Pia, Pia, he holds lost children

in thrall riding all night, yanking reins of his hair
done up in pigtails. At daybreak or dusk,
you may catch their eyes flashing on the horizon
as they charge across the coastal
hilltops and slopes . . .

Dry River Crossing

(St. Vincent, 1993)

In the Mesopotamia Valley,
Althea's household lives under constant threat of flash flood
   or volcanic eruption. The least earth tremors
or word of heavy showers on the mountain sends the valley folk
      into evacuation frenzies.

Just last month, a few mild rumbles spread fear to all valley
            homes—everyone trying
to fill tubs and sinks with water at once,
   packing clothes and stringent necessities to be poised
  for quick exodus. On average, five or six
     such false alarms occur per year,
       but those *volcano drills* keep all families
       primed for the real lava blow off
         whenever it arrives.
       In seventy-nine, during the last big eruption, thousands
         were saved; few laggards lost.

But flash floods strike
with great frequency, and so little warning. Or none. *Rabacca*
  Dry River. Totally dry, today. The river basin,
an oddly pocked and cratered sandy waste, is arid like desert
      outback, but for clumps

of damp mud high-piled, here and there, an ominous reminder.
        Dry can be deceptive.
Heavy damp hangs in the air. River delta
   reeks true scent of this furrowed site—the more dry
   the Rabacca, the more overdue it becomes
     for next minute's surprise flash
       flood . . . The gravel road we traverse for miles,
       while we approach dry wasteland, falls

away to rutted dirt
and muck of riverbed itself. We bounce and dip. A few bucks
could take out our Mazda's

axle at slow speeds
I fear, this island's Minister of Roads and his corps of civil
engineers fighting a losing battle with repair
of the river crossways, no funding to build a proper footbridge
or elevated auto

thoroughfare. Our wheels, from time to time, are snagged by river
bottom gunk, fallen
jetsams. Twice, we get bogged down in debris.
   I jerk the car rocking to and fro, as in our Illinois
snowdrifts, and wobble us free. *Such foul-up*
      in crossing even the near-dry
         Rabacca! Fancy trying to barrel on through,
      says Althea, *when the cataract*
         comes spouting down
         from the mountainside . . . Now she points across the valley
            to the narrow canyon

and upsweep of crevasse
in the distance. Sun may blaze, just like today, no cloud wisps
      anywhere in view, but worst torrential showers
can be raging in high cliffs—those upper rocky reaches obscured,
            totally, from notice

of the shore. *Just so,* she wails. *And from that narrow divide*
                  between mountain peaks
      the deluge comes hurtling down, thirty foot deep,
         perhaps dragging a brutal cargo of uprooted tree stumps
         and loose fist-sized pebbly sludge (upchuckings
            from rock slides, small avalanches
            a daily commonplace in those remote summits) . . .
            All this mad hodgepodge of detritus—
               mossy logs and campers'
               gear, old mattress coils, auto fenders, broken pot shards—
                  is pitched down the swirling

maelstrom, at once . . .
She keeps glancing, nervously, up the far canyon, as if half-
    expectant that her unguarded words may taunt
the demons of the sleeping Rabacca and bring the inundation,
        beset with whirlpools

and great swells of surf foam, cascading fast upon our heads
        at any moment. Now she's
picking up staticky word from the ham radio
    she carries loosely strapped about her neck—and tuned
    to the channel broadcasting weather crisis
      bulletins—that fierce morning
        downpours have steadily pounded the hilltops:
      we've a thirty or forty per cent
        chance for flash flood
          today, but there's no telling when or if it may unleash.
        Rabacca Dry River sleeps,

        nearly always empty,
its waters depleted for months at a time, while most people
    forget the constant threat, relax their vigil,
and the river comes back ever meaner, digging a wider channel
        with its furious claws.

Each year, the riverbed expands at its slow relentless pace
        like a huge black sand
desert basin—and what a mystery it is
    to survey this landscape of absence and ominous retreat! . . .
    We are nearing the far bank, soon to reach
      a high plateau called *Overland*
        safely lifted above the inchoate Rabacca.
      But Althea keeps one eye trained
        on the distant gully
        all the same, while she painfully recalls horrid images
        of that one great flood

        she witnessed firsthand
as a child of ten. She and her grandmother, crossing the bone-
    dry river bottom on foot—following eight months

of unseasonal drought, putting most citizens off their guard—
                              climbed this slant bank

to high ground, just as the cataract broke from those cliffs.
                              They heard a few shocks
and rumbles, before any sure visible sign
    flickered at the limits of sight. Perhaps a dozen men,
    spray tanks on their backs, were fanning out
        over the wide valley—hoses
            spattering the multitude of banana crops
            with fertilizers and pest killers
                (today, all such crop-
                    dusting quickly dispensed by that single one-engine
                        aircraft parked at the edge

                        of a shrunk airfield,
        its runways installed beside Rabacca's many-notched shoreline);
            a long fuel tanker filled to capacity with petrol,
    resembling a motorized centipede, was crawling on sixteen wheels
                        across the riverbed,

when the gusher billowed over the whole sweep of farmlands
                                and desiccated pasture
like a tidal wave. The Dry River's shores
    were no least bar to the rushing deluge, its breadth
    three or four times wider than Rabacca's
        ever-widening deep channel.
            She and Granny clasped each other, safely
            at a remove on the bank, upraised,
                too dumbstruck to wave
                    or yell warnings to the men, hooded with canvas masks
                        and hauling those bulky

                        cylinders on their backs:
too cocooned in their headgear, alas, to hear any shouts, or see
        the flood's wicked forward rim bearing down on them.
She watched eleven of the workers being picked off, one by one,
                    neatly, as though linked

in consecutive ranked formation. The leading edge of water swell
$$\qquad$$seemed calm, near placid,
but a fierce inner roiling of currents
$$\quad$$was revealed by the somersaulting of each field scout,
feet thrown upwards, spray tanks sent flying
$$\qquad$$like so many tubular balloons
$$\qquad\quad$$to all sides. Not a soul dreamed what hit him,
$$\qquad$$floundering in that morass of tumble-
$$\qquad\quad$$weeds and mixed flotsams.
$$\qquad\qquad$$They thrashed their limbs and howled, as if being sucked
$$\qquad\qquad$$into some gelatinous

$$\qquad\qquad\qquad$$primordial ooze, no least
semblance to swim strokes in their apoplectic frenzy. Not one man
$$\quad$$resurfaced that day, most carried far out to sea . . .
Next, they saw the fuel truck slowly tipping over on its side,
$$\qquad\qquad$$as if all but weightless

like a Tinkertoy car, wheels spinning madly, the oil storage
$$\qquad\qquad\qquad$$torpedo vat revolving
at last, soon burst apart on the shore rocks,
$$\quad$$flames surging high overhead like a geyser of fire—
one quick red-orange spout whirling skywards,
$$\qquad$$then *poof!* A slow sputtering out . . .
$$\qquad\quad$$Now came the worst shock, seared into Althea's
$$\qquad\quad$$memory beyond all else: a distant view
$$\qquad\qquad$$of Aunt Edith bowed down
$$\qquad\qquad\quad$$on her knees at the seashore, her back to the advancing
$$\qquad\qquad$$tumultuous wave front

$$\qquad\qquad\qquad$$while heedlessly dunking
her laundry in spring waters near the inlet, humming church hymns
$$\quad$$over her scrub board when that bubbly lip of water
flicked her away like a gently swatted fly. The fingers of foam
$$\qquad\qquad$$that swept her aloft

had seemed almost kind, relaxed and easy, as if coaxing her
$$\qquad\qquad\qquad$$into flight. While lifted

bodily and hurled into the air, queerly
   still scouring her bedsheets, did she suppose she'd
   grown wings—hatched into a great seabird
     or angel? She didn't fight it,
       but opened her arms and reached out to embrace
       the flashing sea fire. As in Sunday
        church choir, her spirit
         drank—freely—whatever was offered. *This, too, must be*
           the light and the reward.

Embracing the Sisserou Parrot

1.

Here, a light mist of rain
seems perpetual. Blazing sun and no cloud wisps in sight . . .
Even the sprawling town of Roseau,
though it cuts a wider swathe
through dense woods
than any other hamlet, is still engulfed in rain forest:
the whole country
a floral garden bathed in constant swifts & runnels.
Only a wee niche
here, a niche there, cut into nature—the Great Sea
of flowers abides, petals & blooms
nodding from every alcove

or recess . . . *This city could be*
a fragile accident, whose
modest towers
can't hold lush vineworld
at bay . . . Today, I'm so inured

to the steady fine shower
of sun-spray, I'm caught by surprise when rain barrels down
in gleamy sheets: I huddle in a low
archway, muttering to myself
about the weird mix
of the elements: torrents and furious downpour paced
by fullest sun
blaze. No wonder, then, flower blossoms seem to spring up
from the very dust
of pavements: they don't need a crack to root down into—
like air plants, they may drink, directly,
from the laziest breezes . . .

Amazed, I keep up a self squabble:
hot rain & cold sun, O how
do they mix
& match? I'm trying to mumble
my way toward sly trope to take in

this potpourri of the sky's
droppings, when a gay whimsical voice overhead (true genie
popped out of a bottle) filters down
three or four stories to me:
it means the Devil
be taking a bride. And I shamble indoors the next moment,
while four hefty
gongs are struck with steel clapper in the bell tower
above my skull:
so near, each peal throbs my spine as if a tuning fork
running down my lower back vibrates
my whole chain of vertebrae . . .

2.

Bowed over, I peer
into the dim-lit Methodist church and take cautious
steps down the aisle.
I catch a pattering of rapid-fire
footfalls linked in winding descent from the tower
three stories above—
so airy and light-footed, they may signal a child's
approach; but no, it's a smallish
graceful black man,
his eyes afire with his lips' broad smile, one hand
outstretched in greeting.
Forehead sweating profusely, he's almost
two heads shorter *than me,* but no dwarf or midget,
just small and fitly

proportioned. I see
          beads of sweat roll down his brow like heavy balls
     of mercury, and fall—
one by one—to his shirt lapels.
               It was I who spoke before. You couldn't see me
                    in the window shaft
               above. The Devil is getting married: that's what
     we say when strong rain & bright sun
          clash. It happens
               every day, here in Roseau. I thank him, Julian
     Walsh his name. Lived
in Chicago for six and a half years,
          until masonry work ran out (no one alive mortars
brick upon cool brick

any faster than he,
          or neater); layoff gave him time to tour the States,
     then homeward bound
to his birthplace: Dominica,
          his secure post saved in a local construction firm
                    pending his anytime
          return. Now he's back in his element, will stay put,
his first home his best love still,
     at thirty-eight. He loves
          the wide spectrum of flowers in every shade or color
     you can possibly dream up—
he may never wish to leave home again.
          God's Rainbow came down to earth in Roseau, says he,
and here it nestled

into the countless
          roots and petals of flowering bush, shrub, orchard.
     You can't walk far,
anyplace in this carnation-choked
          land, without stumbling into the medley of blooms.
               That said, he leads me
          down a narrow aisle between pews to the altar stand,

a great tall flower vase centerpiece
      displayed thereon . . .
            Cheery Anabelle, her arms cradling two thick bouquets
      of fresh-picked long-stemmed
blooms, enters the chapel by a side-door.
            She flicks a perfect white lily to Julian, coquettishly,
and sorts her two choice

clusters of blossom
            in a succession of wall-hanging baskets. Delicately,
      she weaves a few stems
into wreaths around wickerwork rims,
            then stacks the remainder in surprise eye-fetching
                arrangements, no two
            near alike: her knack for sorting by color and shape
a true art. She saves the prize longstems
      to add to the altar
            centerpiece, removing a handful of blooms which show
      first signs of wilting
or loss of freshness . . . Now Julian
            offers me a priapic golden heliconia, bananaesque
in the arc and texture

of its half-opened
            bud, most petals still hugging the sheath. I motion
      to refuse the gift,
shyly, but he insists that I pack
            this one favorite *wild iris* in the journal book
                I carry. It, too, shall wilt
            and die, so he'll have to discard it on the flower-
dump mulch pile back in the churchyard.
      Far better it should
            adorn my note taking in these first euphoric hours
      of my return visit . . .
As Anabelle ducks out the side door,
            she nods her approval of lily stem tucked in my cover,
& dips into a curtsy.

3.

Volunteers
we are, says Julian:
Anabelle comes every third day
to replace all withering flowers with pristine
newborns, then to improvise
fresh patterns
of display. She tends
her baskets, punctually, for a month
or two—then rotates
the task to some other grateful parishioners
of *The Faith.* Julian, who fulfills
both roles of sexton
& janitor

(unpaid as well), will devote each Saturday
all year to the job.
He so proudly takes to the duties.
And greeting pilgrim
visitors
from abroad he finds
to be his gladdest boon. All others,
before him, put in one month,
no more—he the first
to effloresce
into the long-term commitment.
O I'm a hanger-on,
he whispers, playing down his outsize gift

of Spirit.
A diligence . . . Now he's
teaching me the names & shapes
of flowers, the altarpiece an unequal balance
among three varieties:
pink lilies
mostly; a very few
white lilies, the latter soonest turning

drab gray and frayed
around the edges, the petals wilting quickest;
and those dark yellows he dubs
wild iris . . . He commands
my eye

utterly, while he leads my glance, wordlessly,
with his finger wand
from each basket in the equidistant
chain of hanging gardens
to a lovely
sequence of stained-glass
windows, a little above and behind
the neatly suspended bouquets.
Each corresponding window
seems mated
to the flower clusters below.
Proud, proud of these
he is! The windows are less than a year old. . .

4.

A free gift to the church,
he says, from those *rough-and-tumble* American missionaries,
three elderly ladies from Missouri
who vacation here for some weeks
each summer's end.
And what a marvel it was to find them at daybreak,
if not before,
taking hammer and saw, chisel and wrench, to install
the frail windows
in those uncertain frames where cheap dime-store glass
had been poked out, wicked glass slivers
needling their fingertips

and wrists, despite the canvas work
gloves Julian entrusted to them.
Insisted—over
mild protests—that they wore,
as they planed rough edges and pried

old cracked flaky shards
from the corners and pits in yesteryear's window caulking.
He worked alongside, though quicker
they were, and more attentive
to perplexing details
of the hinges; women who devoted more time, he surmised,
to crochet work
or knitting than carpentry. He'd kept the first-aid kits
poised at the ready,
but they hated to stop for a *mere scratch.* The spurt
of a true puncture wound shook one lass
to a halt—briefest at that.

Ageless in their spunk, the Missouri
gals installed twelve windows
below: six
on either side of the main hall
and Chapel, plus four door-size high

swinging windows, ranked
at equal intervals of ascent in the tower. Those windows
in the belfry are *the cat's pajamas,*
he sighs. No one has ever before
built any to compare.
Those below, as I can plainly see, mirror the colors
and petal shapes
of flowers heaped & sorted in the baskets underneath;
while those above
portray true replicas of Dominica's national birds,
the Jaco & Sisserou parrots emblazoned
on the small nation's flag.

5.

His eyes open wide, ever wider, as he burbles,
the art work of prisoners
tagged for life sentences—a grim few
on death row staring down
EARLY DATES
for lethal injections. . .
The rugged all-weather garbage haulers,
house movers and longshoremen
(who loaded & unloaded
Mississippi
barges, the dingiest muscle-
cramping travails)
in their prejail stints: so grateful were they

for solace
given them by those church
women who visited their cells, weekly,
and steeled them to face their *un*futures bravely,
they volunteered (as does Julian
in his way)
to fiddle with jigsaw
glass puzzle pieces, and thereby to groove
their own immortal
Soul Life in Church windows. They cracked sheets
of colored glass into nuggets—
lopsided triangles,
rhomboids,

semicircles—whatever colors & oddly concocted
shapes might seem to match up
with designs of flower bouquets in photos
that Julian sent them
highlighting
a recent flower arranger's
caprice. A few men set out to slavishly
imitate petals with glass parts.

Soulful others devised
fetching twists
that caught the feel of the photos
but took account
of glass shine's own demands. Glass medium stole

their hearts!
The idea of bird-tail feathers
or flower blooms prompted the impulse,
but a mosaic of glass shards made its own claims.
They struggled to appease
both muses,
equally. This I can see,
today, as I compare their window glass
art with the floral
counterparts. No one urged them to be *artists*,
or as imagination dictates,
to create freely—
but rather,

to make fit emblems with colored glass to stand
side-by-side with fresh bouquets.
They gave and gave, unstinting, to glass
flower parts, glass bird beaks,
bird crowns.
They cracked glass sheets, drew
lines with glass knives, and broke zigzags
along the exact seams, precise
and intricate. Mistakes
grew rare.
The windows, cut minutely to size
for the church's
wall grooves, were shipped whole from Missouri

State Prison
to Roseau Methodist Church,
certified and insured, in museum-sturdy
fine-art crates. Julian would love to meet them

all, some lucky day before
they die, or
before *we any of us die*,
to thank them for the gift of their last
months alive. He'd love
to lobby for their *stay of execution*. Well yes,
if Missouri's state governor
came to visit Roseau,
our Julian

would labor to reprieve those *wrongful deaths*,
to commute the wrongful ever-
long life sentence. *O what more proof!*
he asks, that a criminal
has redeemed
himself, than *gifts sublime*
to a foreign land's humble church windows.
And the artists, alas, don't get
to sign their surnames
on their work.
So these immortal glass mosaics—
like aged tapestries
or medieval embroideries—will stay anonymous.

6.

O come, see the Missouri prisoners'
tribute to our endemic birds . . .
I follow Julian
up the winding narrow stairway
into the tower. At each half-flight

of steps to the topmost,
third-story belfry, we stop to inspect the stained-glass
bird door, a swinging gate window
that opens outwards to bestow
full standup view

from window ledge of the world beyond: vistas I relish
of the far seashore
and high foothill cliffs leaning convergent upon the city
as I step, warily,
aloft—stooped on each wide stone window sill, in turn,
and grappling the notched plaster lintel
at my head level for support.

Always, I hesitate to place both feet
on the sill at once. But Julian,
standing beside me,
his head now well below my waist,
chimes, tinkly-voiced: *fear not, it's*

quite safe to step out
and take in the whole sweet panoramas. He doesn't lift
a hand for leverage, but fraternal
voice will do; if human speech
could be translated
into poles and dowel rods, he gave me backup ladder . . .
Now the Sisserou
parrot, pieced together in its glass jigsaw colors, stands
at just my height.
As I grip the window, out-swung on its wobbly hinges
for a moment, I start to lose my balance.
Ah, I should never look down,

only up, out and away . . . I fight off
the temptation to clasp Julian's
shoulder; instead, I
pull the stained-glass Sisserou—
my twin for size & width—to my breast.

I can almost whiff scent
of his glass-inlaid yellow and orange crown of feathers.
Julian chuckles, as if he misreads
my panic—my embrace of the glass
secret bird Soul Kin—

as impulse of ardor, not dread of heights. But my head's
                              swimming with vertigo;
        his smile's erasure is cure . . . I step down, then wend my way
                              up cramped staircase
              to the last window foot ledge, four in number, arranged
                    in a diamond aslant the tower's circular
                                        upsweep. Each bird door swings

              upon a lushly diverse vantage of city
                  or seashore. And when I shuffle
                      into a fourth window
                  station, I'm lightheaded & easy—
              the glass bill and claws of the Jaco

                          parrot tucked in my armpit
            whispers boldness to my thighs, and I swing out so wildly,
                              even Julian grows cautious and tugs
                  me back into the stone wall frame
                              as we chat, randomly,
        about the beauty of roofs, fort towers and stone piers
                      only half-visible
          through the translucent sheen of perpetual sun showers.
                          No matter how thin
              a veil the mist of constant rain provides, it distorts
              and adorns the view, always shimmering
                              with new facets, new glamours . . .

                Julian, yanking on the bell rope, rings
                  five sharp peals of the next hour—
                      singing, once more,
                  the Devil takes a bride, takes
                a bride. O the wedding of sun and rain!

II.

Wide Skull, Puffy Jowls

So-Han places one hand under my chin, the other
 flat against the back of my skull,
 and squeezes, gently;
 his two palms
 a calipers taking my measure—I'm clamped,
 my back slapped
 to the museum wall, my forehead
 just inches below
 the anaconda's propped-open
 jaws, eternally

frozen in mid-bite. The twenty five foot corpus,
 stuffed & mounted, winds, sinuously,
 back on itself and fills
 the whole wall
 panel. *O my head's too wide to fit between*
 those jowls, say I,
 for all their touted skill to stretch
 balloonlike & engorge
 their prey . . . But So-Han, who leads
 teams of hunters

on bimonthly treks to Guyana's dense interior
 in pursuit of game fowl, spotted
 wildcats, hogs, baboons,
 & constrictor
 snakes to supply the Georgetown Zoo, pooh-
 poohs my demurral.
 As he passes his palm over my most
 imposing skull bumps,
 his voice flattens each bulge,
 in turn: *Big Snake*

has all the time in the world to wait for head
bones to soften up and collapse
on their marrows. He
and his *mates*
while away sultry days hidden in the bush,
stalking a queen
anaconda and her nested brood—
whereupon they await
the return of her prime bull
for capture. Queeny,

meanwhile, may preoccupy herself with adjusting
the carcass of a just-strangled deer,
a full-size adult buck,
say. She smooths
& flattens, smooths & crumbles bone shafts,
shrinks the dead
deer in its hide. Spitting her acids
from time to time,
she'll soften the hard tissues
to pulpy masses.

As she stretches the limbs & haunches, the deer
rearranges itself in its sack, all
bulks shrunk to pancakes
of flesh-and-bone
mash. *Our skull, that toughest nut to crack,*
is left for last.
But it, too, spreads out into some fine
amalgam of flat
grist—in time, even her babes can
swallow us whole.

Spine

At an outdoors
rural cafe, the few tables
scattered over a wide glary courtyard,
we four the lone lunch
guests at this late siesta hour . . .
I shall be first
to sample dear native cuisine:
Creme de la Iguana
Soup. So far from a clear broth,
as I'd mistook,
I find my utensil
tapping a succession of antlered
horny bones, tinkly,
like a xylophone's many keys.
As I lift them,
one by one, from the bowl's
lower depths, vertebra
after flared vertebra—I ponder.
They seem graduated by size
to match up
in a simulated human backbone.
Never before did I fancy
a lizard's skeleton
so close a kin
to my own neck and spinal
segments. No chicken, duck, or turkey
necks ever struck so keen a chord
of unwelcome
kinship! I gulp my fake
approval, taking smallest sips.
O let the others get on
with their serpently bones' confection,
while I muddle

and snuffle my way from tail
to narrow brain case,
spoon by gritty spoonful.
I fancy I
must be squirmily turning back
the clock on my own
lame evolution,
returning to my slime of its slime,
layer after layer,
mire unto slow-paced mire.

The Iguana Hunter's Floating Gait

After lunch, Franz
springs to his feet to salute Otto,
this year's top-ranking
iguana hunter. Otto tilts to one side,
long narrow face
sporting a thin line Rudolf Valentino mustache—
who now basks
in Franz's boastful tribute
to his gifts of the stalk & pounce.
A tall lean presence, Otto bobs, ever so slightly

on balls of bare feet,
forward-leaning, a praying mantis:
his jointed-stick arms
floated outwards, twiggy fingers up-curled—
poised at the ready.
His buoyant moves, as in a dumb show, eerily
punctuate Franz's
tale of the hunt . . . Most days,
off goes leggy Otto on his thick-tired
bike, humming a relaxed tune. In an hour, he sweeps

back from the bush,
his double baskets weighted down
with two dozen
thrashing and roiling brawny lizards:
iguanas of all sizes
loosely tied, two-or-three to a plastic sack.
A few creatures,
contorted in mad heaves
to burst free from their tethers,
are folded double upon themselves. Fiercely coiling

and uncoiling
in confused whipsaw of torsos,
they may crush
small cousins beside them . . . Otto keeps
most of his lively
catch *undead,* for sale directly to housewives
and chefs—iguana,
like lobster, best flavored
when cooked alive . . . Franz has seen him
at work in the bush, slithering down on all fours

like a possum,
or shinnying up a tree trunk,
noiseless & quick,
with fewest slinky moves. He may employ
forked branch or lasso
to snare a head or tail in motion, but mostly,
bare hands suffice!
Otto's the only Bonairean,
on record, to have snatched two iguanas
from tree limb roosts at once, grappling the lower

one by the tail,
the higher by its fat belly,
while the furtive
male was performing a courtship ritual
over the female's
head. Those wriggles & shudders—mating amours—
kept both players
distracted for mere eye-blink lapse
Otto needed to bring off his two fisted
strike . . . And now, even as we speak, Otto hurtles

three steps forward,
then hangs poised on a verge. We hold
our tongues, to hear
him intensely listen. How does he process
the silence, splitting it

up into tiniest rustles? Now we stare *with* him
at a large mottled
back, near-shrouded from view
in grassy sedge, lurking just beyond
the wide courtyard margins. As our hunter commences

his slow dream glide
upon the basking sun-lulled creature,
we hear two chaps
making whispered bets against a barmaid's
smug promise: "Otto'll
nab de Big Guy—never fails!" Her idol drifts
a few steps, halts,
still more steps, again quits,
repeating this cycle five or six times.
In pauses, he plies breath insucks, like skin divers

hyperventilating
before a plunge. *Light breaths, ever
lighter.* Heartbeat,
in turn, retards—his pulse slows and slows.
Floating his last steps,
Otto primes for the chase . . . Iguana's head darts
from side to side,
snout lifted above the grass
cover. He, too, listens hard—his senses
envelop the full surround. Body radar? Perhaps it's

a true third eye,
centered at the back of his head.
With it, he tracks
skin auras, whether flowing from humans
or other hostile
aggressors. But fooled by Otto's slow heartbeat,
he drops his guard,
snapped up firmly under the jaws
by three-fingered trident grip. Otto swings
convulsive flesh tube overhead . . . *A Victory Pennant.*

Shaggy Mane Lord

Just overhead, on either side of the aisle
two great yellow bulks
seem braced to spring upon me.
O why am I stalked
indoors,
no jungle? I only
half-believe I'm in any danger—
for that brief eye flash . . .
No imitations
or fakes,
these two lions—male to my left,
female poised opposite—
are trapped in moments of wild ferocity

& hunger,
loud hunger for me
as I try to run—but freeze
instead: their long teeth exposed, jaws
dropped open in what
must be
operatic howls.
Were these two Golden Beauties
snared and butchered
in their primes, then carted back here
from West Africa, still looking
their most bloodthirsty
and regal ,

I muse, *just to petrify the likes of me*
dumbstruck in my tracks?
For a protracted two minutes
I'm as paralyzed

as they—
we nod to each other
like Egyptian Sphinxes, stone face
to snarling yellow-whiskered
face. Stone to stone.
But I don't
die of fright . . . Now why, I ask,
is this golden husky's
grandeur, O lovely verge of spring & pounce,

its life peak,
squandered for a museum
display? Why snuff out the Glory's
breath, and falsify its bone-and-skin bag
into this life-mocking
Stuffed Doll
Colossus? . . . For years,
they were Guyana Zoo's *class act*,
says plucky So-Han.
The biggest drawing card for school kids.
Our Lena was more than halfway
to her first litter:
three whelps,

at least, were incubating in her hot box
when Rasta Pluto fried
his brains with too much hash.
Sir Lion is my Guru,
he muttered,
hoarsely, to anyone
near the beast cages who would listen.
He sounded like a high priest
hailing the new
Messiah.
Big Spirit, no cage can hold
him back. He boundless.
De jungle's inside him, no taking it out.

Duh Revolt
come soon, be ready,
my shaggy mane Lord will say
his piece. His wake-up call be coming.
Police grinned, and looked
away. Pluto
fiddled with his dreadlocks.
Slept two nights by his new Savior's
cage, chanting mantras.
On the third night, our Rastafarian fled—
throwing the watchman off guard.
But just before daybreak,
he crept

back under the gates, a puffy sack hidden
in his shirt. He took
sledgehammer & chisel, then burst
open the padlocks,
setting free
two golden-haired thick-pawed
Majesties, to roam the night city & maul
whoever should be taking
their good health
of predawn
stroll . . . They chased Pluto, for all
his pains, up the nearest tree,
ripping off a pant leg and part of one shoe.

The pair led
a gaggle of police
on a two-hour chase through farmer's
market, parochial school grounds and soccer
stadium—whereat a sniper
nailed one
high in the bleachers,
the other behind the goal post
(while the field of play
and stands, luckily, were vacant), a big-time

playoff tournament scheduled
for later that day.
They dragged

off the dying carcass by their tails, Leonine
Royal Carrion slopping
muzzle blood and guts on fresh-cut
turf, and on front rows
of box seats,
the wide trail of innards
zigzagging down the chalk-white painted
centerline . . . Soon both teams
would be mystified
by ground
smears and gunky mothball-sized clots
choking the grass: telltale
marks of postgame riots, carnage of embattled

soccer fans
inflicting juicy mayhem
on one another. But why, pray tell,
wasn't the blood bath reported in the media?
And why hadn't groundskeepers
tidied up
during the day-long
interim? All news broadcasts
of fugitive lions'
assault on three joggers, two near-fatal,
and resultant police shootings
of the zoo's star breeder
couple

were held back—at first, to prevent panic,
and later, to spare police
ignominy. *Bad form, those gun downs,*
So-Han dryly laments:
far better
to have roped & captured

those valuable beasts unharmed . . . Alive,
both creatures were worth
double their weight
in opals . . .
On the museum plaque, rare species
named, Africa origin cited—
no hint of melee that led to their slayings.

The Chinese Gambling House

(Paramaribo, Surinam)

No lofty high rise
in view, the Capital is *wood proud. Wood ablaze of color.*
This oldest all-wood
city in the Americas, for all its poverty and debt,
keeps its many varicolored balconies
and shop fronts freshly stained & polished, like so many soldiers'
boot toes lined up
in formation. I scan the urban skyline.
The few Islamic mosques

stand out. Pinnacles—
wildly angular and geometric—curlicue the far horizon.
Tower tops, like giant
pinwheels or corkscrews, jab and skewer the vistas.
Strolling toward the shipyards, I glimpse
the distant riverside—then pull up short before a surprise Asian
greathouse. Set back
from the main drag on a triangular island
looms the much-buttressed

four-tiered mansion,
brisk traffic buzzing past in three directions. Poring over
wide florid house face
and arch of entryway, I study the giant Chinese brass
alphabets nailed to the lintel overhead,
then dash between thick spurts of motorists, and step up to the gate.
A lone black boy,
seated on the porch rail, makes quizzical
squints at me. *Owlish*

eye poppings. He knows
he's out of place, but clings to this margin, a tame renegade

                                    at the ready to split
                  from here, if rebuked. His stare pulls rank on me.
                    Even less than he, it's clear, do I belong
          in this odd satellite of the Ming Dynasty. But I shamelessly prance
                                        past him, and cross
                      the threshold into some displaced Orient . . .
                          At first glance, a blur.

                                        Dusky, the ground floor
              is a blank waste, tunneled by two hallways of boarded-over doors.
                            The immense atrium,
                  a wide empty arena, cuts a three-story-high shaft
                      through house center. It could be a defunct
      storage depot, fallen into ill repair from disuse, then perhaps sold
                                        to Chinese mafia
                    warlords, the bulk of the building shut down
                        indefinitely . . . I cavort

                                        up a dark staircase
          drawn to brittle clickety-clacks, and find myself installed
                            on a wide balcony
                  overlook that affords a fine glistening vantage
                      of the bustly avenues and far riverbank.
      Some few guests, lolling and musing on canes, are bowed at the window
                              ledge, and I'm weaving
                    to and fro between a myriad plushy lounge chairs
                          or rocking divans, most

                                        occupied by sleepers
              or aged Chinamen smoking long curled pipes, ornamental designs
                              engraved on their bowls.
              The air is drenched—replete with incense and pipe smoke
                      musk . . . I gasp my way across the veranda
      to three inner rooms, heated board play in progress in each: all tables
                                steamy with arm swings,
                      the frenetic players men of middle years slapping
                          those thick colorful tiles

on echoing tabletops,
no women in the affray. But young Eurasian dolls, who hang back
from the fumy gambits
never daring to coach the moves or wavering strategy
of stakes, chime their hurrahs and jeers
to match the wins and losses of their favorite tile jockeys. And it *was*
a horse race, of sorts,
since tall odds were bet against the underdog
at each table, or so I

surmise . . . *Detroit*
nostalgias flare. Myself tagalong and meek cheering section
for a trio of aunts
who placed high in city-wide mah-jong bouts, I stood
at their elbows, my forehead just even
with the chair tops, and proffered solace to the Dame whose chip pile
had dwindled to six
or fewer, chanting screwball victory slogans
to the budding winners.

So many gnats, gadflies,
mopers, or gigglers, we nurslings were indulged, if not held dear,
at those mah-jong fests.
Our hostesses were accidental baby sitters, ourselves
their parasites or pawns, whose input
was tuned out by all parties; but nonetheless, we fancied we had *pull*—
and even tilted,
magically, the fate of the tiles with our sighs
or groans . . . Ah, still less

visible do I feel
today. Impalpable, I might be a tattered pennant of white smoke
in rolled-up shirt
sleeves and egg-smutched collar. It's a closed circuit,
but inured politeness forbids the gamblers
giving me the boot. I'm a fleeting nonevent. If not for thick miasma
of fumes and mist trails
stinging my sinuses, I'd doubt I'm here! *A saving*
pipe ash grazes my lip, . . .

Work Chants at an Abandoned Gold Mill

1.

We stand, shakily, on an exposed
wall top. Dead center in the capacious ruins
of the gold smelting plant. Julio,
pointing to each hallway and corner in the mazy
labyrinth of unroofed rooms,
lovingly details each stage of the smelter's

art—from raw ore
to ingot, as if he'd stood, side-by-side,
with the last factory teams prior
to close down
(1914, the outbreak of World War I) . . .
Next, he motions
over his left shoulder, tracing scars
of deep ravines: those open pit mines,
half-hidden, all-but-emptied of any slim lodes
of ore, stretching perhaps a full quarter mile
behind this smelter works.

*The gold mill, gold
extraction plant,* Julio calls it,
by turns. And he sketches, for me, the multitudes
of men, mostly cheap migrant workers
shuffled—hither and yon—between the Dominican Republic's

copper mines, Venezuela's oil
refineries, & Aruba's gold Mecca, then back
roundabout—across the circuit.
Wherever the boom of the day, the fiery moment,
they'd all rush to join
the marathon work force. Wherever the fever

                    to keep a pace
of chop, drill, hack, or heft dropped far behind
                         production quotas for the Foreman's
                              job detail,
                    those numbers, numbers of men without limit,
                    came roaring *home*
          to close the gap. All souls who'd migrate
                         downisles or upisles quickly enough
          hoped to be paid, feasted, bedded, bonused,
                    and *pensioned* against the storms of age! Ah, such
                    promises drew the great waves

of Carib work
hordes from one fitful haven
     of monetary largess to the next: freed slaves,
     by the thousands, fed their numbers—
     forcibly stampeded in slave days, most held that fervid pulse

                              and rhythm in the postslave
era. The whiff of adventure and steady work,
                    however fleeting, kept the human
               meat market in flux as surely as the moon swung
                    its tides and the reversal
     of sea currents . . . Julio chants! His rumbly voice

          burns with their gasps
and work songs, as scores of halest laborers—
                    of six diverse races and five distinct
                              home tongues—
               join forces in Papiemento chorus: now I
               see them, yet again,
     wrestling those great jagged quartz
                    and limestone boulders all freshly dug
     from mine pits into wagons, improbably sturdy,
                    wheels and axles tooled from *watapane,* the toughest
                    most durable wood in the world.

Watapane, ideal
stock for underwater ship parts,

all-but-extinct today, was squandered by the last
generation. Julio's voice cracks
with sadness, to think of the waste of one more great resource.

2.

The five ton blocks,
rolled across a sloped platform resting on logs,
settle on the steel-based concrete
floor of the mill anteroom. On average,
each metric ton of stone—hacked
& scooped from the quarry—
might yield a mere seven ounces
of tiny gold flecks.
And here, the many-phased process
of pulverizing begins. The plank scaffold,
two stories above,
provides footing for the stout

teams of *crushers.*
Six huge battering rams are dropped, in sequence,
from a thirty foot height. The timbers,
great logs steel-capped like spearheads,
smash the rough-hewn boulders
into smallish rocks.
All stone icicles, slivers,
& shavings, are swept
into piles—basketed and salvaged . . .
Transported in squat wheelbarrows to station #2,
where *grinders*
reduce the size of thick rocks

to small pebbles,
gravelly flak. At times, two burly men must wield
the great steel sledge in tandem,
four hands, linked side-by-side, grappling
the one super-hardwood shaft.
Fierce overhead swings!

Two brute huskies fastened upon
self-oiled resins
of that thick handle, at once—four arms
    entangled before the witness, four shoulders
      crimped in a circle,
      so fast and agile, a magic duo . . .

              At a glance, it's
    a single two-headed spider man at work, four-
          fistedly sledgehammering nuggets,
      the largest stone shards, then dropping
        the smallish bits like so many
                silver, black or green
       peppercorns into the viselike jaws
              of rotating barrels.
      Soon, they are mashed to a fine-ground
  sandy texture, the gritty heaps hauled in sacks
             to an airtight
      superheated chamber, a sauna

      which raises temps
    far above boiling; pressurized steam is pumped in,
wave by wave, while the piping hot sludge
    is flushed down a sloped chute into the first
    of three basement rooms, where a pool
of liquid mercury,
    flame-heated in a deep cauldron,
melts the gold
deposits, casting off igneous waste
    which, dense in mass, sinks to the bottom.
    The thin gold ore
    fuses into particles of a low-

            density alloy,
  Au/Merc, that floats atop the hot mercury bath.
         This precipitate, a film drifting
      on the surface, is caught in fine-mesh-net
        metal strainers and transferred
              into the next pool,

the potassium cyanide bath.
From there, alloys
are piped, sizzling yet, to the third pool,
the muriatic acid bath; each chemical, in turn,
alters the fusion,
loosening bonds of the compound.

These sediments,
at last, are funneled into water tubs, dislodging
gold from mercury. Tiniest gold flecks,
slow dried in evaporators, are collected
with still-finer-meshed sieves.
The pure gold dust,
transported in close-knit fiber sacks
to the bullion
chamber, is treated with more chemicals,
then melted down and processed into rock-solid
gold bars & ingots,
at the ready for sale and export.

3.

Julio, hopping from one roofless
wall-top cross section to the next, keeps me
trailing him. A few of his leaps,
broad jumps from wall to wall, test my scant mettle,
the risk of falls to exposed
floors below me more than fifteen or twenty feet . . .

Ah, I do try
to hang back, but he snags me in tow, I
must be *in presence,* he says, to catch
a true whiff
of that *turn-of-the-century hullabaloo.*
Indeed, each step
of the gold extraction process he
punctuates from our free-wheeling roosts,

above, with much grace and flourish of arm waves!
He puts his own shoulder into that lunge and zip—
whoosh of those sledgehammers;

he grunts and hoots
and whistles the Foreman's commands
to his bare-back crews . . . O it's clear, he takes
an architect's delight in mapping out
diagrams of the many-chambered factory. At sixty-six years,

he can't have witnessed events
firsthand, but he often got the story direct
from the lips of Uncle Vlinders,
the gold smelters' chief marshall, who scouted
from station to station,
from battering rammers to mercury baths to gold

dust retrieval tanks;
who never failed to catch a poacher trying
to pocket some gleamy flat nuggets
or small sack
of the refined pure ore itself: Vlinders
decorated, yearly,
with medals awarded by the plant Foreman
and the island's Dutch governor, alike,
he the holder of first honors in *factory*
security for many years running. Official duties:
upholding safety rules, fire

& flood control—
but well he knew his job survival
was tied to his record for nabbing gold thieves
in the act of pilfering, so many
arrests per month, to set an example for leagues of migrants,

what with that heavy turnover
of new recruits to be trained each week. Heyday
years, these were, of stepped-up

production, frequent layoffs of feeble or laggard
crewmen, many chance goings
and comings of transients from their home islands

at any hint,
or rumor, of better pay to be earned abroad . . .
Uncle Vlinders, too, took young Julio
on this high-
stepping roof hopper's tour: *you must be skin-
and-bone in the thick
of that scene to conjure up the true feel
of hissing bubbly acids when Au/Merc
alloy was dumped in the sizzly brew, flinty sparks
and smoky crackling pots in the smelters' forge,
rumbles of the blast furnace,*

*or those dangerous
outpourings of rock showers,
angular sharp-edged missiles flying anywhichway
when battering ram struck a boulder
dead center of the vein, raining pebbles and fine rock spray*

*on all heads within a radius
of thirty square feet, for long minutes there-
after (stooped skulls duck & swerve) . . .
The glass-visored helmets of squad chiefs were few
and far between, devilish hard
to come by, unless you had* an in *with the bosses' wives.*

III.

Notes from the Synagogue Museum

(Mikve-Israel, Curacao, 1994)

Through the airtight
glass face, I peer at a homemade compact tool kit:
            antique instruments, gleamy on the maroon
plush velour lining. Two minisets
            of scissors recall tiny shears
                        in my late mother's
                  sewing box, but the blades do look
                        suspiciously over-
            sharp and surgical: too short perhaps
to get much snap or breadth . . . Ah, I see a rough-
                        edged nail file
            and delicate toothy tweezers.

                  May these utensils,
then, grace a manicurist's craft? But no, I discern
            calibrated number scales rimming the sides
      of two or three tools—subdivided
                  into fractions for minutest
                        accuracy. Perhaps
                  they are antique calipers & compass
                  of an architect's
            portable rig . . . But the darker hushed
overtones (echoing David Cronenberg's mutant
                        sex forceps
            of the twin-bro gynecologists

            in *Dead Ringers*)
send me hunting for the fine-print caption nestled
            in the box corner: *Circumcision Instruments.*
      And my eye zooms diagonally
            to the authorized manual,
                        a key-pocket-size

text: *The Circumcizer's Ritual Book . . .*
In a flash, I conjure
images of that eighteenth-century
Surgeon Rabbi: the newborn babe laid out flat
& squalling
on one forearm like a violin,

rhapsodic free arm
waving the surgical clippers hither and thither
like the fiddler's bow, while he sings—
moans & davens, at once—CHANTS
from tiny ritual book silk-tied
to tall upright stand
under his chin . . . O look, he groans out
those long-held Hebrew
syllables, hugs the child to his breast,
pirouettes, then pancake flips the he-babe supine
on the altar,
podium turned operating table.

And like as not
when he hits a long high note, cantor-style, *snip snip*
goeth the clippers, our Rabbi never losing
his glad song lilt, nor missing
the beat . . . blood spurts . . . thin trickles
plash, again & again,
as the healer croons his blessing,
laying down his snub-
nosed blades, at last . . . He trembles forth
deep quavery notes, a paean to cleansing. *O wound*
that makes pure
the fount of seed & progeny.

Ladyknife

A chance meeting
        at Statia Airport.
            My last quarter hour chat
            with David Shaw's
cut short—seaplane's last call: *All Aboard*
for Saba . . . His warning words to me, lone traveler,
            buzz, buzz in my ears
            as I mount short ramp to the cabin:
    beware Sabian
        ladies—any age,
            any race—very adept
                they be with knife, so quick to use
blade: tempers flare,

shortest fuses
    of gals anyplace
        in the Antilles . . . Years back,
            Shaw did monthly gigs
with three-piece band (he strums antique banjo,
family heirloom), worked most weekends of Saba dance
            concerts. Near halfway
            through one Saturday's hot tune fest,
    at break time,
        he spotted young lady—
            his pal of three seasons—
            hovering near the hall entryway. Soon,
he bid her cross

the bar doorsill,
    come be his guest
        all night: free drinks, free price
        of admission—she
some flashy dancer, her hypnotic moves filling

dance halls many a slow night; but no way to budge her,
            she stood her ground
                as if an invisible wall of steel
        hung betwixt them.
            She ran, no fond adieus
                lip-wafted, as was her wont,
                    to her friend. Two near gals, sullen,
Shaw quizzed why

Verna, twentyish,
        would balk at October's
                top JUMP-UP. *Police jail threats,*
            they sniveled, for all
reply, until, in due course, he pumped them
for the baleful story . . . Earlier that week, harassed
                on the dance floor, Verna
                    cut up drunk seaman, two slashes quick
        as you can blink:
                took two fingers, a single
                    ear lobe (jeweled ring hooked
                    therein) flying across the bar top
like a baited hook

and leader flung
        in a wild cast. Her blade,
                though short, darting in and out
                like a snake's tongue,
left him flopping, belly-down, on staircase,
fishlike, legs pumping a scissors kick, but who can swim
                up a flight of stairs? . . .
                After two refusals, he'd kept trying,
        roughly, to *cut in,*
                to cleave her—in midprance—
                    from a dance partner; whereupon,
                    spun about on one heel, she took, first,
two fingers dug

into her forearm
        viselike, slashing upwards

with her free hand, and severed
ear gem in the same swipe;
the next, a down chop, split his lower cheek
and caught his inner thigh, flailing away to the stairs.
Two mates hauled him,
shoulder slung, to the hospital clinic;
they patched him up,
plugged leaks in his face
and leg, cauterized ear gash,
but no retrieval of his index finger
or thumb—*moshed*

to shreds in dance
heat frenzy, the band
so torrid nobody noticed raw
flesh slugs hurled
overhead, nor the melee of three tusslers,
their moves less fierce than many high steppers' hot brawl . . .
Constable Corky
gave Verna three-minute standup lecture,
disarmed her, *shiv*
to be held for evidence,
if needed: "It not be me wish
to criminalize thou. I'll waive fine,
waive mandatory

jail term, if thee
but pledge to set no foot
upon these dance bar premises
for nigh three years.
If I sh'd spot yuh hereabouts, I'll stash yer
straightways in de clinker, and toss out duh key. Mi-nee-mum
sentence for knife
blood-drawings be six fortnights!"
Minus time off
for holidays, Queen's
Pardon—at worst, she'd be sprung
in two weeks . . . Coy Verna, wagging her lashes,
won back her knife.

Lament for the Lady Felons

As we zigzag and circle
the castle's base, we seem to be crawling endlessly
                    up a road snake's furrowed back,
                rising some six hundred feet
                            into the cloud-wisp
eagle high-flier's upper air zones: Fort Charlotte hangs
                over Kingstown's Civic
Center and Iron Market, impending from a steep cliff—
                    one-time citadel
            & fortress for the capital city, much touted
            as impregnable to the leagues
                            of would-be invaders.

                Now whichever way I look,
        I'm struck by hard-edged rawboned horizontals, rawboned
                        verticals: dizzying! What a bastion,
            this tower, in ages past,
                            to scare off enemy
ships entering the harbor. A few well-aimed cannonballs,
                    though none hit home,
            might send them oar-scurrying for cover, then back again
                            to open sea . . . We take
            a stroll around the tower battlements, pass some few
                upraised brass cannons, and twist
                            them this way and that

                    in well-oiled emplacements
        still primed for battle, though no invaders have reared
                            their prows for two hundred years.
            But the site reeks, even so,
                            with old enmities,
old wrangles . . . Althea now leads me down a stairwell

to a low oval-shaped
barracks which, she declares, once housed two battalions
of proven scouts
and marksmen, troops of the finest mettle: champions
of their day. But I soon discover,
this sheltered retreat

and hideaway bunk quarters
which slept the men in tiers, stacked two-to-three-deep
as on sleeper cars of a modern train:
this steel-reinforced garrison
is fully revived,
today, for a new civic use. *Prison for our worst*
lady criminals.
Worst case offenders may be confined, here, for life
sentences. Yet no,
I'm assured it is not equipped with gas chamber,
gallows, or guillotine. They stop
short of executions.

Women aren't *put to death,*
but they may be subjected, often, to *moderate* routines
of clever or mischievous torture,
at the mercy of the jailor's
improvisatory whim.
As you might suppose, day guards and their night counter-
parts may widely differ
in punitive measures-of-the-hour, as shall seem most apt
at a special time
of day . . . She cautions me to not step too near
the windowless jail. RESTRICTED
reads the wooden plank

dangled from two short ropes
above the double-padlocked entrance, sole doorway, perhaps,
into the steel frame. *What a sardine*
can, I say. *O how it must stink*
within, since no proper

ventilation seems possible . . . Why not?, she flatly replies.
They brought it on
themselves, don't you know. Poised just outside the quarantined
sector, I now hear
a few high-pitched cackles, whether from pleasure
or pain I cannot say. Those voices
are too muffled—they fade out

and chime in again. *Well yes,*
Althea explains, *five or six women were jailed here, years*
back, the most ever locked up at once,
though this prison's equipped
to hold thirty girls.
Today, both ladies are murderesses, crimes of most recent
vintage—grisly facts
of their wildness still surfacing in the media, at intervals.
The rising voices,
aflutter within, sound like a whole flock of caged
birdy lasses. *No, just two,* Althea
insists—stands by her guns,

and I back off while she
rehashes the brutal gun-down details of your classic love
quadrangle: one mistress shoots boy-
friend in the arms of the other,
both gals *unbeknownst*
to the wife, unsuspecting, home in an eighth-month vigil
of her tenth pregnancy
coming to term. The other lady assailant, packing a small
revolver, robbed—
of all things—a bakery and doughnut shop. Not loot or hard
currency was she hot after, mind you,
but day-old crusts of bread

to feed her seven famished
offspring. She'd gladly have settled for a few stale hunks,
coarse scraps. But the baker resisted
her sputter of flaky commands,

jokily mocking, and tried
to bean her with a flour-smeared rolling pin. Then the gun
tripped off, discharging
in the scuffle. Or so she pled her case to the wry constable
and subsequent court
magistrate. Deaf ears, all—threw the book at her . . .
Why so few lady felons?, I ask.
St. Vincent, this country

of some seventy thousand
inhabitants, surely can provide more worst types—heinous
lady transgressors . . . Oh Lordy, don't
propose such a disgrace, Althea
replies. *Aren't two wicked*
girls enough! . . . But mightn't a criminal lass ever be paroled,
her life term shortened?
I grumble. *Perhaps, but only if she's soon to give birth*
to a prison guard's
baby. Her eyes happily approve this quaint tradeoff—
it's a bargain struck, for the good
of her countrywomen.

The Marriage Furies

                Randall Whyte's great granddad,
a purebred Scotsman, sent his only son, Zachary, to Barbados
                to manage a great sugar plantation, subsequently
appointing his two Scots cousins

                            overseers
                to a trio of lesser plantation estates
in Grenada. The lax cousins,
                refusing to become *expats,* put in
                as residency one summer month
plus a scant four weeks
                spread over the year—then trusting
a broad succession
of local hirelings to stand in
                for them . . . Year after year, the Grenada
                    sugar tracts fell
                    in yield, for lack of hands-on

            caretaking by the absentee landlord
kinsfolk, while those Barbados sugar crops greatly thrived,
                setting annual records for yield & export sales,
owing to the steadfast labors

                        of son Zack, who,
                quietly mating with one ink black daughter
of a just-freed-slave cane worker,
                begot three roly-poly mulatto boys
                in as many years, then a lone
fair-skinned ("passably
                white") *she child.* And not one soul
in all Bridgetown's
elite matriarchy raised an eyebrow,

or cast a slur . . . But on the day he wedded
    his kids' black
    mom in secret ceremony

of the outback (no priest: a secular
low court justice spoke minimum rites to tie their nuptial
    knot), the three story plantation house went up
in flames—just before nightfall—

    set fiercely
    ablaze in half a minute. The team of horses,
wild-eyed, kept trying to bolt
    from the canopied wagon in which huddled
    the escaping family fivesome,
the whitish she-babe
    still suckling her momma's black teat,
while the masked
papa rode the rear horse of four,
    often reining the frantic team to swerve clear
    of homemade bombs,
    that series of exploding bottles

    hurled at their flanks (Molotov
cocktails, or some early variant of such), the frail carriage
    upending twice, near overturned on its rear chassis
during a final dash to the wharf,

    where a tattered
    fish sloop hunkered low for rescue at dusk.
The bandannaed skipper, crouching,
    never hoisted sail until he'd smuggled
    all four tots aboard, two each hid
in a pair of fish tubs,
    a whirling maelstrom of flak—buckshot,
flaming arrows,
small rocks slinghurled—bombarding
    the one-hundred-meter last charge of the horses
    to stone jetty
    and pierside . . . *O, where the pursuers?*

Not one in view! But those batteries
of primitive munitions kept flying from dunes, from beach-side
            hovel, most falling short of the mark, one horse
toppled to its knees by a hammer

                        wickedly flung
                into its foaming snout, the mother's black hair
        sparked aglow by a fiery arrow's
                near miss, as quickly doused, her head dunked
                in surfy brine by the quick-witted
        boatman while she clung
                to gunwale of his crude rescue dinghy . . .
When great Patriarch
Whyte's son emerged, weeks later,
                securely at the helm of those three rundown
                        Grenada sugar
                        plantations, no one had a clue

        about Zack's bedeviled flight
from Barbados. His neighbors, throughout the South Province,
        gaped upon amazing pickup—overnight—in cane field
output: layoffs of laggards,

                        by the score,
                followed by mindful hirings of both skilled
        senior work force and able pickers,
                backed by strong bank credit and capital
                accruing from his Scots' family
        imprimatur: the ring
                sporting his father's engraved seal
as pedigree . . .
Months hence, when wife & offspring
                first paraded their faces at Sunday service,
                        no least stir
                        ensued—thanks to his sugar fiefdom.

Three Years after the Four Days' War

I'm met, hot off the plane, by suave Ferdinand
who runs the vanguard fleet
of cars for rent.
Silver-thick mustachioed, neat
as his goatee, luminous blue shirtjacked,
spiffy, urbane: he could be president of the bank
or majority whip
in Parliament (a youthful seventyish), but he leases
cars, trucks, mobile homes—
and small efficiency kitchenettes
to American
students of the Medical College. Their landlord,
yes, but I soon learn he's surrogate father, guide,

much adored caretaker of his whole fraternal
order of guests. Well met,
soonest parted:
I'm given over to wise counsel
of son Terry, mild proprietary chum
who mates me with car of my choice, then offers
to shepherd my vehicle
to insiders' safe-and-frugal sea-view guest hostel . . .
Still in my first half-hour
of Grenada jet touchdown, I pop
the big question
to Terry. *How did you and your family regard
the invasion ASSAULT by our U.S. Marines?* His reply

comes forthright, without pause. *You won't find one
Grenadian who does not love
your America
for the IN-TER-VEN-TION.* He drawls

the four syllables of that neutral word
with emphasis on each accented drawn-out vowel,
blunting, utterly, the sting
of my charged come-on. I back off, at once. So we chat,
idly, Terry's subdued voice
muffled by the rising pitch of Marie, Lill,
his two daughters,
ages eight and five, tagalongs for the diversion.
The battle of small wits, a jokey vocal duet, evolves

a chain of shock words and images, while I struggle
not to reveal my drift
away from Terry's
genial pep talk, warmhearted,
palsy with clues and tips for sleuthing out
the best local music, cuisine, sports events, and O
Romance! . . . But the back-seat
snippets of inspired babytalk take a turn that pangs
my ears, chokes up my breath:
one moment, the chatter is party favors,
dolls, baby bottles;
next moment, with no shift in tone or tempo,
the palaver alters to sophisticated war verbiage,

war lingos. *Greenish-blue cannon fire. Mortar shells*
spitting hails of shrapnel.
Gouge-wounds. Scars.
Limb amputated in front yard,
decapitated skull *whirled like bowling ball*
across the lawn. *Blood spouts plugged, flows stanched*
by bandage or tourniquet—
in nursery or parlor, not once in hospital unit or ward.
Street gunslingers *moshed*
this enemy, that six-year-old child
punctured in random
sniper crossfire . . . Papa in front-seat so inured,
all flies past, his ears grown immune to verbal canker.

Hosting an Idol

          His status reversed
  overnight, from traitor on death row to populist
      hero—both roles illusory and deranged—Senator Winston,
          just three months
      out of prison, kept to the sidelines of life;
          but he found himself
playing host, if passively, to *a bloomin' galaxy* of heads
          of state from three continents . . .
  also a handful of writers and artists. His heart rose, finally,
          at the prospect

          of stewarding
  an idol, great favorite author of his school days,
      V. S. Naipaul, whose rep as chillingly aloof preceded him.
          On first meeting,
      Win found him magnetic, as if a great ball
          of luminous energy
surrounded his person and swept everything he touched,
          everyone he met, helplessly,
      into its field. And in the weeks of Naipaul's visit that ensued,
          Win often felt,

          eerily, he could scent
  the man's nimbus of excitement in the air currents
      of street life, whenever Naipaul—with or without entourage
          of fans, groupies—
      approached, say, within a four block radius
          of Win's chance stroll
or dallying course. The stir, like as not, was prompted by Naipaul's
          unorthodox style of cruising
      in heavy traffic, so eager he was *to gad about* to all ends
          of town. Local folks

spotted him, daily,
zooming the wrong way down narrow one-way avenues
on his outsize Honda cycle, bullet silver racer's helmet
bent forward & down
like a bull blindly charging the matador.
If Win came upon him
combing an area, he'd pick safe recess, well back from corner
or curb, for cool-eyed surveillance:
at times, V. S. resembled a hot rodder burning rubber to convert
St. George's congested

pier-side street map
into a roulette table, or a video game space duel
of the rocket ships: the map was *his* to conquer, the game
play a wizard's
whirligig route, traversing all main arteries
with the fewest shifts,
or turns, between points. His passion erupted, a breathless contest
to sleuth the whole territory,
leave no shop front unscrutinized, while most pedestrians,
mounted horsemen,

motorists, or fellow
cyclists in Naipaul's wake, were spun about in their tracks,
at a loss to decipher his madcap course of spins and swerves . . .
In those first days,
they clicked like soul buddies, Win so agile
in his efforts to steer
Naipaul back in line from his fierce vehicular overbite, glad rage
to gobble up every person
or locale he encountered; and it was worth the fevered pace
to share that high

pulse of adrenaline
which V. S. engendered in everyone he met, or grazed.
It led Win to ponder that style of art and lifemanship,
a pent-up furor
lest some *one* pungent tidbit of experience

be missed. Even so, Win
essayed to relax and calm his new friend, by indirect suggestion:
the moves of Senator Winston's
long-limbed spare emaciated carriage, when the gabby pair
took walks together,

swing of his arms,
the slow halting pitch of his hips—these counseled V. S.
to wind down, take island life calmer; nor ever spoke it out
in audible voice,
heard words too much like a scolding, so it worked!
Win molded a spell
of quiet diplomacy between them. *A trance. Power held in restraint . . .*
So soon after the upheaval
and tumult of the invasion, Grenadians in marketplace
and street arena

took special umbrage
at Naipaul's manic streakings hither and yon, who
seemed every place at once. One woman, a senior bank teller,
declared she thought
she saw six clones of this man. *How, otherwise,*
could he find himself
in so many parts of the bank, there was no time for him to scurry
from wall to wall, cubicle
to stall, he was three different kinds of mirage—quivered,
vibrated into a blur,

then flew apart,
or broke up into separate frames and skins. In time,
he became the choice topic in local street jabber, everyone
trying to size
him up in words or exotic images; but no one
quite took his measure,
this man who came to garner raw materials, fodder for a book
he might put *them* in. Instead,
he left them all befuddled, feeling more than a little abused,
but not sure why.

The Morning Star, Extinguished

(Trinidad, Summer '90)

1.

Nicole Rugallah, thirteen-year-old dusky
      Trinidad Muslim,
    my seat mate
on the LIAT shuttle flight, her great aunt
      and cousin seated squarely
    behind us—
today, they embark on a crisis mission,

      voyage to Curacao . . .
    Foragers,
they would gather a few scarcest provisions,
      household staples nowhere
    to be found
in Port-of-Spain, what with squalid lootings
      and all day curfews.
    Open markets

have been *pillaged and torn asunder,* food shops
      torched to ash or rubble
    (Nicole's speech
peppered with suchlike Biblical flourish),
      in the course of two weeks'
    frantic plunder.
As necessities grow more dear, the rioters

      fan out from the Capitol
    to far suburbs,
invade the small-scale family groceries,
      then storm the diners,
    cafe kitchens,

for rice, grain, any perishable foodstuffs;
        while today, the renegades
    are singling

out private estates and homes, for assault.
        Luckily, Nicole's homestead
    is miles distant
from the city outskirts; so far, no looters
        have breached their family
    threshold, rude
poor folks' dwelling in a township of paupers.

2.

Abu Bakkar, that heroic Robin Hood among Muslims, supported
        by his small band of followers,
    took over the seat of government for many days—Nicole recounts.
        They shot Prime Minister Robinson
in the leg *(by accident, I beg to assure you)*
        during the scuffle that ensued when they struck the Capitol,
        taking Robinson and his cabinet
    ministers hostage; they made their few demands,
        then held steady . . .

Nicole and her sisters find themselves trapped, shopping
        in Port-of-Spain, at leisure, when,
    without warning or siren, many people swarm in all directions—
        frenzied pileups at the shop doors,
    many getting crushed underfoot, or pinned in doorways.
        Shooshed into the streets, they climb through half-open low
        windows, unhurt; guns discharging
    on all sides, so close, they see pistol flash
        & smoke, flare-ups

in the sky like lightning. They hail a cab, grim half-hour's
        breakneck charge beyond the suburbs
    to their shantytown: *the road bumps pained we bones,* backs & necks
        achy for weeks afterwards. Home,

their parents' eyes are glued to TV for bulletins,
                the whole island on WAR ALERT. Lights grow dim, then BLACKOUT.
                        Two minutes later, power returns:
                        Abu Bakkar looms before them on the TV screen,
                        a Muslim God

risen to greet the Rugallah household, for themselves alone
                        a private screening—so fancies Nicole
        in those first moments of relief. Fleeting comfort, at best! Bakkar
                chants the coming of a *New Age.*
        Your prime minister's been shot, a minor flesh wound
                to the leg, his cabinet is detained, the army must surrender
                        to indomitable forces of the coup,
                        Robinson regime is bowed down, the whole leadership
                        held hostage,

remain in your homes until further notice, or you may be shot,
                        Capitol's under full siege, we
        are the new government, stay tuned to this channel for all update
                        bulletins . . . Her family is cheered
        and stricken with fear, by turns: their folk hero
                seems ascendant like the Morning Star, but food's in short supply
                        and water scarce, cistern levels
                low from months of drought, and they harbor
                no prospect

of fresh provisions into the foreseeable future, who ration
                the few victuals with utmost care . . .
        Today, weeks later, Bakkar and his troop stew in municipal jail,
                upshot of that sudden showdown.
        One pistol-toting civilian house painter, runty
                of stature, still costumed in his rainbow-bespotted work clothes,
                        broke onto the scene, trapped Abu,
                and the rebels all backed down . . . But Nicole,
                unwavery

to her last breath, holds firm, confident Bakkar's cabal
                will be set free, no judgment
        enforced against them. *They shan't be martyred,* or the citizens
                will rise up in protest, the wave

of popular support quickly toppling Robinson's
            regime, that terrible leader who—year after year—has *suffered,*
                suffered the poorest classes.
            For seven years, mounting numbers of people
            have starved,

whole families of her friends thrust into the streets to beg
                food, the most basic resources
            denied them by the ruling junta: *apples and grapes, fresh apples*
                and grapes, always her first food love
    in recent years, never slipping past the boss party's
                embargo to the common people, while the upper class minority
                hoard all freshest fruits. Still,
                Nicole is hopeful. Last week, four countries
                came forward

with aid programs, big shipments of food and meds arriving,
                daily, from Barbados, Jamaica,
    Venezuela, and even Guyana. It must be proud Muslims, she insists,
                who march and rally in the streets
    to coax their leaders to donate food crates, gift
                boxes, to her crippled nation: *PROOF,* she says (in subdued murmurs,
                I must bring my ear up close
            to her lips) those Muslims in helper republics
            are in league

with Muslims, worldwide, to support good Bakkar's rebellion
                in Trinidad. And soon they'll win
    Abu's release, then pull down the Robinson power block. Her eyes
                ablaze, she fully expects a multi-
    national invasion force of world Muslims to stage
            a holy uprising, a little Armageddon of the sea isles, to rally
                behind Bakkar, and thus, raise
            her ethnic block, the Muslims of Trinidad, to proper
            rank and station.

Farewell to the Lost Music Scores

1.

Whenever we meet again,
you'll recognize me by this white hat, Shaw's
                  parting words—
he bustles out the door of COOL CORNER, his hat a cotton
soft knickknack flopped down anywhichway on his silver-
                  bristly scalp, all borders
drooped evenly over his brow and whitish sideburns. So ends
our first whirlwind fraternal chat, he perhaps always blurrily
                  tousled & frantic
to hop quick between stops. Today's crisis
may be offbeat, but his glandular tempo's revealed, an innate
cartwheeling life rhythm,

                  his boyish elfin thirty-
         year-old daimon trapped in a seventyish (or late
                  sixties) physique.
He still composes music with the scratchiest quill pen
he can find on yellow-bordered antique music staff papers
                  turned up at the corners,
fray-edged, or he can't bring himself to whisk those first
brave notes of score. *Got a happy wire this A.M.,* says he.
                  Unexpected news
         cabled. Some three short romantic choral pieces
he'd penned, months back, were performed—to great ovation—
on Rhode Island radio,

                  just today; he to wire
         reply pronto by return cable, granting permissions:
                  world rights

for repeated broadcasts on National Public Radio and Voice
of America's syndicated Music-to-Four-Continents. He balked
            at the *perpetuity clause,*
grumbled, then wired his HURRAHS . . . Shaw loves to recite verse,
short ribald poems by Lovelace or Herrick he's set to music,
                cranking up
        the humor, lest some listeners miss that *bawdy wit*
shrouded by a veneer of fake sentiment. I try to pump him
for career milestones

            of his musical youth.
        Shyly, he turns mum . . . Avid naturalist that he is,
                he'd delight
to teach me a vast spectrum of flowers, arcane tree species,
rare orchid phyla *nobody's yet dreamed of,* unnamed still.
            But later. This morning,
he's running to the tune of his young Statian wife (her first
nuptials, his third), two vagabonds who've been bottled up
                in pigeonhole
        third-story apartment for this whole past year,
a menial dour flat. Their louvers, but grudgingly, let in
least whiffs of sea gust,

                still less light, dormer
        windows angled the worst possible way to catch
                blest trade winds.
No help for it! When married just six months, they'd lost
their ancestral house to fire (arsonist still at large)
            while they dallied in Saba,
Dutch sister isle, on a three-day holiday. Sad farewells
to his rare book library. Farewell to many autograph scores
                by his composer
        peers & forbears, those priceless hand-me-downs.
And farewell to Shaw's best creations, *uncopied* choral gems,
crowned by his avowed

masterwork: *The Snake*
Prince, ballet of six years' fruition, tailored
to unique blends
of myth and history espoused by his beloved dance troop—
Ballet Martiniquisais. No matter, he'll reconstruct
the bare-bones of his dance
score from memory. What a yarn of rhapsody and sorrow,
alchemy and enchantment! He must frame those scenes, yet,
for the premiere
troop to *trip out* that wondrous tale on stages
in Fort-du-France . . . David's whole frothy bent of person,
I see, is raw genius

to build back from loss—
loss of youth, library, inspired music scores,
family habitat.
The passion to begin again, it's all one happy challenge.
The survivor revives . . . And who, I ask, set his house
on fire? Well, nobody knows.
Of course, there are always rumors in a place so small,
where jealousy, rivalry, & revenges abound. The lucky man
walks in fear
to step on his own shadow, unless he be poised,
ever poised, to lose everything. And welcome it . . . Today,
Shaw's in house-builder

furor, his little Nissan
piled high, bags of mortar and cement protruding
through sun roof
gap. He'll ferry every load from wharf to budding homestead,
hammer every nail himself *from the ground up,* if no help
be forthcoming. But his gusto
rouses volunteer helpmates, lend-a-hand idlers from field
or town square hopping on his caravan unasked, unbidden;
yes, so I discern
as I follow his trail to the village environs,
and come to know how his small-boned frail birdy carriage
rages to begin again.

2.

Naturalist, bibliophile,
ballet master, choral composer, and himself fair-
voiced chorister,
he was active in church choirs since a boy soprano, age six,
at Rhode Island parish. Surely, he gave his pedagogues
one better than he got back
from them, in turn, at each step of the voyage; likewise,
his gifts to me, today. *Alas, no time for a proper visit,*
says he, at bus stop,
airport stool, lunch counter, but he exchanges,
fiercely, bits & cross sections of talk. I walk away richer,
for each near miss

of a visit, near scrapes
with his transient pizzazz: our parting word my
name inscribed
in a copy of my latest book, keepsake for his new library.
I fancy his wife, perched in their third-story walkup,
jolly & confident—in time,
Shaw and that chance succession of aiders shall patch
together the new house, layer by layer, shingle by louver:
no rush, a build-
as-you-go life process, luck comes, luck goes . . .
When Shaw recites passages of favorite verse in English,
or Creole French, and when

he rattles off synopses
or few-word-chain-link digests of island tales,
true-story Carib
novellas, I know a true bibliophile's library shall never
be reduced to ash, though bindings be shredded to fluff,
all print roasted as pages
furl, scroll, and smithereen away into the fire-roar winds!
His best love's Villon, whose verse he sings with a passion
sublime, akin

to our late James Wright's freewheeling recitals
from memory. Now I notice his eye corners, a frolic in wink
creases. Therein survives

      those eraseless residues
    of his adored seventeenth-century comic laureates'
        never surpassed
love jokes, the gamy love dalliances of Herrick, Lovelace,
Marvell as alive here today—on this remote Dutch territory—
      as in any library archive.
No book burn down can vie with Shaw's chants, word-voiced sighs,
or his tongue-tip's archly lingering refrains . . . Just once,
      he lets slip,
    Bach's, always and evermore, his soul mate
music maker. But for all the great writers of ages past, none
takes his breath away

      or electrifies his pulse
    quite like the Caribbean's own unsung hero, Labat.
      Who can believe
such a Renaissance human comet as Father Labat?, he quizzes
the unanswering winds. No lost treasure was held more dear
      by Shaw, following the blaze
that incinerated his library, than Labat's *QUARTET:* a mint
first edition bearing the author's scrawl, the complete works
      in four volumes.
    Poet-priest, surgeon-naturalist, and *our era's*
most gifted graphic artist, his *illuminated* books contain
lucid anatomical drawings

      for all definitive species
    of island fauna, bestiary given true-to-life *feel*
      as never before.
A secret Michelangelo of each lizard, each insect, Labat
renders detail with a loving quiet eye that rivals God's
      own sweet bounty of creaturely
color and design. *Ah, such ardor he brings to the telling*
of each bony or fleshly appurtenance. Go—without delay—

                    to Fort-du-France,
        Shaw commands me, *while extant copies of Labat's*
glorious QUARTET can still be acquired only in Martinique
for a mere $200 U.S.

                The letter-press gilt quarto
        edition, never to be reprinted perhaps, grab it!
                Iguanas, I declare,
are so incisively portrayed, their luminous joints, necks
& tail segments seem to catch light, hold it, then flash it
                back at you from the glowing page.
They may surpass the originals! And I, for all my book loves,
music loves, like Prospero, feel most at home in the wilds.
                Today, I'd love
        nothing better than to take you by the hand, sir,
& lead you to each rare island species . . . But my wife waits,
I rebuild our chateau . . .

IV.

Thirst

Who dug these many botched channels,
scoopouts in the desert terrain? . . . Scores of half-dug
    wells, abandoned at all stages
            of production, disfigure the lunar flats
in South Bonaire, the land gouged with six-foot-wide holes
            that resemble minicraters
of the moon. There may be
    three or four such pits per acre,
        the shallow tunnels beneath veiled

        and near-plugged with a hodgepodge
of debris—old rotted logs, rusty fence wire, misshapen
    stones: local *well-wishers'*
            attempts to protect the isle's many sheep,
goats, and wild donkeys from falls into traps below; human
            strays, too, adults *or* infants,
those curious wayfarers,
    local citizens and outlanders
        alike. Many signs and telltale clues

        reveal that the multitude
of unfinished wells were hacked, chopped, drilled, shoveled,
    or poleaxed, intermittently,
            across a wide time frame spanning perhaps
four hundred years, or more. The rare completed wells, still
            yielding their bounteous gallons
of fresh pure spring water,
    lead us, yet again, to puzzle
        over those numberless failed tries—

        no written records, but a few cave
drawings may provide the answer. So many brave diggers quit
    too soon: what scared them off—

typhoons, wild boars, poison snakes? . . . Bonaire's
low-lying hillocks conceal layers and layers of grottoes, cavern
           upon cavern, some caves so shallow
only a small child might crawl
      through the low fissures, clefts,
            at either end of limestone hollows.

           Others are wide high amphitheaters
carved from the overhanging rock, topped by a frail shell
      for roof, perilous to climbers
                 and diggers who might fall through to crushed
limbs, or instant death. Well diggers, breaking through cave-roof
                 crust, grew squeamish, chary to risk
their necks to sudden plunges.
      But in driest years, the few inches
           of rainfall shrinking to fewer—squaws

           & babes howling for drink, that chorus
of parched throats kept the well scouts plying their tools,
      hacking and scooping, despite
                 mortal risks: no injury too painful to hazard,
in hope to slake that multiplicity of thirsts. *Starts and stops,*
                 rife across the land. Why so many
false onsets, so many abortings? . . .
      On one cave wall, two rescue teams—
           pictured above—lower buckets of food

           to fallen mate, rope ladder dangled
to hoist victim digger, crack-boned or hale, back through cave-
      top gorge. But other grim murals
                 reveal horrors feared, dooms foretold, surpassing
all fleshly hurts. Overhead, the rope snaps, severed on jagged rock,
                 letting a half-hauled man plummet
into abyssal deeps. Below his legs,
      do we not see hairy-knuckled claws
           scoring raw flesh of foot soles, insteps,

and yanking the toes? Horned heads
drool, flashing smirks—demons of the Underworld, these, who lie
　　in ambush for souls of the fallen.
　　　　　　Three or four cave layers, at most *(O narrow*
margin!), buoy our soul's dance to recover its footing, then elude
　　　　　　the reach of those grasping talons
and slavery fangs . . . *Ah, far better*
　　to endure all earthly droughts than risk
　　　　our soul bait to glut those fiendish thirsts!

Urn Burial

Elise, seated in a dingy
candle-lit corner of her family crypt,
more a storybook dungeon
or torture chamber to her eleven years
than holy tomb (housing
remains of four generations of her Papa's
Dutch clan), cradles
her granddad's exhumed skull in her lap.
She stares into those scoured-clean
eye sockets,
entranced . . . Franz, busily transferring
his disinterred sire's
bones from the first-burial coffin
to a knee-high ceramic urn:
secondary urn burial a custom
of the Caiquetto Indians on his mother's
side of the family tree,

he would make room in the elegant
hand-carved coffin
for his elder sister Melanie's corpse,
three days dead, a stout ample woman
to the last, and, as always,
needing her space . . . Elise chants,
in low murmurs,
while Franz, noting she ticks off
numbers with fingers of her right hand,

then the left, and back again
through the cycle, supposes she counts out
the lapskull's twenty-four
afterlife years, mostly years before the day
of her birth. A child who
never met her granddad before this death-in-life

tryst in gloom
of the family vault, she seems to brood
　　　　　her elfin spirit further back in time,
　　　　　　　numbering the years,
　　　months perhaps, on the abacus of her hands'
　　　　small knuckles; much as she
likes to count backwards from one hundred
　　　　　to zero, and far into the minus
column when she jumps rope after hours,
　　　　　a prayerlike ritual begging her mom to extend
　　her bedtime a few last jumps,

staying up for dear life, forestalling,
　　　　　　　ever, the last minute's
　　　　presleep countdown . . . Tonight, Franz diverts
himself with fitting his father's
　　　　　long bones—paired femurs
& tibias, radii & ulnas—
　　around the urn's
　　　　high concave neck with utmost care,
vigilant to leave room for the rib cage,

　　　　　　　still intact, wide hip bones
and consecutive vertebrae of the spinal
　　　　column, saving for the last
a near-spherical gap in the urn's top, dead
　　　　　center, for the Crown Jewel.
Franz puts off to the last possible instant
　　the sad onus
of barging into his daughter Elise's
　　　　　silent colloquy with the skull bones
　　　　　　propped between
her knees: still, she rattles off computations,
　　　now tapping the numbers,
finger by finger, on the loose jawbone,
　　　　　that faraway look in her eyes
the transport of one who augurs
　　　　beauties, or horrors, in the years to come.
Her father bids her to pass

him her prize, the hallowed vessel
                              of her ancestor's
                  razed brain, for reburial. And as she lifts
              that bone case to him with both hands
                        cupped, gingerly, beneath
              the erstwhile chin (now missing
                    those puffy jowls
                              she'd once perused in the family
    album), he risks a joke about her math

                              jugglery: is she counting,
        he asks, the long tally of her unforgotten
                    male and female progenitors;
              or keeping tabs on the sheer number of bones
                  he'd shifted from coffin
    to ceramic vase? *Finger & toe digits, small*
                  as snail shells.
    Hip & shoulder bones, round and curled
                  like the chambered nautilus.
                        Much quantity
              of spinal vertebrae, knobby and antlered
                  as elkhorns of finely
          graduated sizes, small to large to small,
                        tracing the scale from neck to seat . . .
        "Oh no, Papa," she replies. "I was
                  counting Granddad's teeth, every one in place,
              not one molar or wisdom tooth

    lost, in all his eighty-six years, while you,
                        but half Granddad's age,
                  retain no more than four upper teeth, six
          lowers." "Aha!" yelps Franz. "My father,
                  schooled in local plant lore,
              cleansed his teeth, from babyhood,
                  by chewing fresh-
                        picked branches of the Stockie Tree."
    Poor child-age Franz was cursed with dentistry.

The Legend of Rode Pan Well

Rode Pan Well, one
of the oldest on Bonaire, was a favorite
watering hole for the slave
hordes plodding
those nine hour treks
to visit their families on weekends
in Rincon township—
brief respite, alas,
from the marathon
workweek at the Solar Salt Ponds. This well,
midway in their grueling hike,
never failed them.
Come, you must sample

Bonaire's freshest
sweet well water, says Franz. As I lower
the two-hundred-year-old
dyewood bucket,
I catch fleeting
glimpses of my face, starkly mirrored
upon the surface
below, while clean-cut
edges of ivy leaf
bestride my ear, ivy stem sprung from my hair
and roped about my neck, ivy
looping wildly
around the well's rim.

It waits in ambush,
to choke the glary-eyed narcissist who
feasts on his own image.
A faint mist

puffs up, which blurs
my lips. Thick smoke gusts from hidden
vents, now lower,
now higher, keep drifting
from side to side.
Lord, those smokes have swallowed up my face!—
took first the eyes, then
mouth and nose,
saving for last my jaw

and ears . . . The afterimage
lingers in smoke half light, but that mirror
is cloaked: *myself de-faced*. Franz
finds me in stupor,
primed for the Legend
of Rode Pan Well. *Waist-bent here*, says he,
the wise old slave
taught those slave youths
to know true worth
of their souls. In loss of freedom, they'd win
the prize jewel of spirit,
forever missed
by the White Possessors.

He who has no name,
no past, owns no earthly goods (not even
the anonymous hemp or burlap
potato-sack rags,
smeared on his back),
shall find himself brooding, long and long,
into this deep well.
And if he but stare
at his blank face
staring back, he shall watch it fade—at length—
to mist, and then pure void.
The midday smoke,
thickening, will rise.

And when it climbs
over the well rim, it may cover his eyes.
                    Blinded, he speaks to the hole.
          They buy and sell
                    me   they take away
my face   now I have no more face to take
                         O but they miss
                    the real of me   it
               stays and stays
later, they'll come back to ask me, faceless
          how to die   for they forget
     (so encumbered
                    with gain)   when, where, or

                         howsoever to die
they have many faces   maybe two for each
                    pair of eyes   but how can they
          know if they live,
                    so afraid to die . . .
As his voice trails off, smoke puffs abate.
                    And soon the hole
               in the well clears. My
          image returns,
staring, trance-eyed, in the glassy black water
          below. I shut my eyes, grope
     for lost white mien—
               O face behind my face!

The Origin of Stars

An hour early,
we await our secret Cabal, a midnight tryst
with Pa Francesco, retired astro-
physicist who fervidly kept publishing
for six decades. Yet when he turned
eighty in 1980
(born at the turn of the century,
his auspicious birth
no accident, to be sure: itself
guided by a rare conjunction of stars), he gave
over science
for spiritualism—the prize

of his life's ninth decade! This spring,
with the advent of his tenth ten years, comes the rejuvenating
of his youth's lost innocence . . . Cloudless. No trace
of mist. A ghostly starlit calm

full-moony night.
At the exact appointed site in blank desert,
far from pathway, road or human
dwelling, we squat between the Mystic
Five Rocks, and muse . . . One minute
shy of twelve sharp,
the new-fledged nonagenarian
looms before us wobbly
on his mule, the pair so quiet
we heard no clop of hooves, snort or snuffle.
Has he trained
his dull-witted beast to take

silent steps, *silent breaths,* a trick
with the reins perhaps? At stroke of midnight, pale Francesco

lifts his tall stovepipe hat (bright diagrams
of the starry galaxies inscribed

                              on both sides,
luminous-green inked: his Merlin top hat, gaily
              he calls it), and waves the brim
         in circles overhead, while chanting
            vague oaths and Latinisms
               to the unlistening
         stars, never budging from his perch.
             Franz and I stoop,
        bewitched, poised for the arrival
of two giant rams with golden horns. Will they drop
                 out of the sky,
       leap from the nearest cave mouth,

  or be ejected whole from a subterranean
grotto, its fissures suddenly cracking open beneath our feet?
    The rams, it is foretold, shall do a jump-up
dance, perhaps flying so close

                     to desert sands
one must stare at their wildly prancing hooves
        to discern *they do not touch earth* —
      never quite scraping the sandy plain
        they skim cross, though puffs
           of dust be stirred,
      whirling, from the little cyclones
          they shall make
      with their frenzied legs & haunches.
They'll back off from each other, at the last, rise
            on their hind legs
        in stately furor, and then race,

  snorting, one upon the other, with lowered
gleaming horns. When those golden antlers clash and interlock,
  sparks and glowing particles shall be thrown off
by the friction, some fading embers

falling harmless
at our feet. But high-flying sparks may hover,
as if becoming new fixed stars
in the firmament. And so, we hold vigil
for a moonlit dance and battle
of two shining rams
with golden horns, as was prophesied
by our top-hatted
conjurer, mule-propped and hallowed
in his ninetieth year . . . But alas, no such glory
comes swirling
into our desert ken. *Why no show ?*

we ask Francesco. *You must believe harder,*
says he. *Be more foolish & empty, to be filled with best faith.*
Then your rams will come, lock horns, and send
sparks flying to hatch into stars.

By the Light of One Star

Stooped, we enter the cave of the petroglyphs.
Reddish, a dried-blood
    color, the swirls of paint are derived
      from volcanic ash, which bonds its glaze to coral cave walls
    for a near-permanent fix.
No one has yet decoded some of these portraits,
    while most figures—animals, warriors, or holy men

              garbed in tall headdress—
    are starkly clear to the untrained eye. *Ignore*
        the bolder orange marks scrawled
    below, dotted
      and broken, says Franz,
my guide for the day. *Graffiti imitations. The botched*
    work of vandals . . . Next,
    Franz zigzags
down the path to a more secluded cavern,
    leading me into a half-dark
    spacious high arena
      in the rock, whereupon

    he bids me to stand at ease in a central pit
and stay in place,
    peering overhead, while he exits
      for five or ten minutes to prepare *a demo* for me. In time,
    I hear Franz's remote voice
muffled high above. Then I see a crack of light
    overhead, which widens swiftly into a quarter-moon,

          half-moon and full-moon shapes,
    at last a blazing hole in the cave-roof dark,
      Franz having removed the rock

cover from the cave's
natural round skylight
in abrupt shifts, three dramatic stages to create a surprise
lunar simulation. *Stay*
where you are,
he shouts, his scowling-jokey mug framed
by the bright circular gap,
face shrunk to a waspy
grimace at that height.

Now I can just hear him scrabbling on all fours
back down the rock pile
he'd climbed, slowly and quietly,
brief moments before, until I find him puffing at my side—
in two minutes flat. *Behold,*
the Mati Mati! And it *is* a tantalizing sight,
a near-perfect ring carved into the grotto's concave

roof. *That shining mouth*
through the cave top has always been there,
but we keep the close-fitting
stone plug fastened
upon it all year round,
Franz avers, *to protect wild goats and donkeys from slipping*
on the rim (so curious
they are, if sure-
footed usually), and falling down the slot
to their deaths on limestone
shelf below . . . For seasons
numberless, his ancestors

chanted myths foretelling the yet-undiscovered
Mati Mati of Bonaire,
who knew it would be detected in our time
by one keen of eye and blessed with power to read the stars.
Such was the Simacan, who,
finding this cave with the traditional roof aperture,
studied the stars and predicted the very hour, minute,

of the hallowed night
when that one brightest star would cross
the magical ring, and gleam
in dead center,
thus casting enough light
to throw a luminous wide rondure on the cave floor below—
the unearthly radiance
seemingly brighter
for these two or three minutes each year
than light of a full moon.
Just one star, one star!
Those standing in or near

the ghostly circle would be blessed with a power
to dance and sing
the dying old year out and, moments
later, to cheer the New Year in . . . Others, before Simacan,
guessed this cave might harbor
the one true Mati Mati prophesied in early myths.
For many months, each year, they posted relay teams

of all-night sentries, who
vowed to stare into the roof gap every minute,
most vigilant to discover, first,
the one bright star
of the night intense enough
to cast the historic shimmering circle on the limestone
cave floor at their feet.
Eagle-eyed watchers,
they fancied themselves, but at the crucial
moment of that sacred hour
their attention flagged:
the glowing orb slipped by,

unnoticed . . . Not one sentinel ever chanced upon
the pulsating lone star;
though each year, faithful to its mission,
it shone dazzlingly at the appointed time, none but the blind

or faithless there to behold
its muted glory. After years of failure at the watch,
        it may be they lost the will to believe in one fateful

                                star. Who are we to judge
                their efforts? Oh, such constancy in staring
                        at the heavens, the starry cosmos,
                for a beacon light
                        message—does it not require
        a steadfast faith to sustain it? And that bold staying power
                was the visual acuity
                or mental sinew
        of the Simacan who, yet in his thirties,
                after ponderous study
        of star clusters
                circling above this shelf

        of cave grottoes, mapped out the trail of one star
he tagged—Mati Mati.
        Poring over his graphs and charts, he called
        for a select gathering of his fellow shamans upon the night
        of December twenty-second.
Pressed close, they stood in a huddle below the roof slot,
        some few armed with very intricate and expensive fold-up

                                spyglasses for the event,
                not one expecting the vivid charge of a Mati
                        Mati Star. So soon it would come
                sweeping across
                        the circular dark vista
        like a pointy firebrand, a fiery knife point of light,
                at the precise instant
                that glad Simacan
        had prognosticated its arrival. They dropped
                their rudimentary scopes
                in astonishment—
                        for any soul among the troop

blessed with sufficient vision to see his own hand
upraised before his face
could easily witness that glory, Simacan's
fame secured for a lifetime . . . Since that day, all devotees
of the local mythology
and faith gather in this cave under the pillar of light
on the twenty-second evening of December, to see out

the old year, then usher in
the next. The original shock of that first day
a fleeting sixty-three years ago
lingers, ever,
in this bare cave arena.
It still has the same power to lift our hearts and stir up
our wonder, avows Franz,
much like the impact
of a full solar eclipse on untold thousands—
viewers rudely camped out, say,
on hilltops of Hawaii,
Brazil, or Mexico City,

having traveled great distances from home, perhaps,
to secure an ideal gape
at that sublime conjunction of astral bodies.
Likewise, crossings of that bright star may strike fear & joy
in our souls at once: the cave
so dark one moment, you can't see a man beside you; the next,
he's illumined as if he holds a lit candle under his face.

Ballad of the Star Hijackers

Years back, when the early U.S.
satellite Sky Lab commenced, prematurely,
its slow descent through earth's
ionosphere, there was a great buzz and stir,
a placing of bets, even,
by global bookies: guesswork as to where
the closely-watched-
on-seven-continents premiere space probe
might touch down. Would it drop
into the sea?
Or hurtle upon a land mass, its contents
to be preserved
and scrutinized by the host country,
then costlily ransomed for secret
transfer back to America . . . As Sky Lab
fell closer and closer to fast-burn frictions
and gravitational pullback

of our atmosphere, expert hunches
about probable land-or-sea drop sites kept fluctuating
hourly—the papers and TV
were riddled with maps and diagrams
charting coordinates for Sky Lab's final plunge, gale force winds,
or storms of small consequence
until that swift white heat
plummeting through the stratosphere
to our bottom layer weather systems . . . Throughout

the final week, Pa Francesco,
retired astrophysicist of some renown,
kept tracking the satellite's
course. Still elated by his budding new career

in paranormal and occult
science, Francesco smugly reported to Franz,
his young disciple,
that he had found the answer to Sky Lab's
riddle. Her Black Box was destined
to fall first,
in Bonaire, the satellite's principle mass
to be delayed
for a sizzling flamedown in the forests
of southern Australia. Franz nodded.
Then, Pa implored his protégé to take
a journey with him in the dying satellite's
cockpit . . . Apt time and place

fixed for their seance in the starlit
desert plain, Franz hoisted some few barrels and cartons
of spiritualist gadgetry—
electrode tubes, ultraviolet
ray lamps and portable battery-run power rigs; then, together,
they unloaded and assembled
the *Space Travel Kit.* While seated
for hours on the flat ledge
of a sacred volcanic rock, their concentration

on Pa's list of magic numbers
kept them in laborious trance—punctuated
by a vivid sequence of colorful
flashing lights—toward the appointed Space/Time
nexus when Sky Lab was slated
to revolve directly overhead. And true to a stop-
watch's millisecond,
some three hours and seventeen minutes
from the time their vigil had begun,
Sky Lab passed
immediately above Franz's upturned brow.
The next moment,
it seemed as if a galactic tongs
composed entirely of stars came down

(Sagittarius, centaur-and-archer,
             is made of stars, but what a difference to us—
       who be prone to peer and dream

over his sprawling shape—if he were
to let fly, suddenly, a feather-backed arrow from his bow),
       snatched both Franz and Pa Francesco,
             gently but firmly, around their middles
and deposited them in Sky Lab's cockpit, seated behind the radio
             feedback mikes and main telescope—
prior to this moment, strictly
       an *unmanned* space vehicle . . .
             I ask Franz, at a momentary pause in the tale,

             if they were *bodily present*
in the rotating cage, or was their transport,
             rather, just *out-of-body travel:*
       their hurtling spirits carried around the globe
             while their deep-tranced mind-
emptied physiques lay dreaming, or *dreamless,* say,
       on the flat-topped
desert rock. *No way to be sure,* says Franz,
             though he remembers they slapped
                   each other's
       cheeks sharply enough to bring tears of pain
             to their eyes, tears
       they could see falling on the satellite's
             instrument panel; and Franz bumped
his left knee so hard on the ship's compass
       wheel, as he tried to lift himself high enough
       to get a full clear view

of the entire African continent
when they spun wildly over Nigeria, he found he was cursed
       with a painful limp for weeks
             afterwards. But these body data
are not unimpeachable, since, as we all know, we humans are given
             to play such odd body games

in our dreams, pinching ourselves
          to prove we are awake,
                    then embracing our newly revived dead mother

                              or father with a palpable
intensity and firmness, sufficient to defy
          any such absurd passing fancy
          as we may be fast asleep . . . That the two men
                    had been cozily nestled
          within the revolving egg cannot be doubted,
                    whatever human
     parts—if any—may have been left behind,
                         supine on the bald rock below.
                                        Franz recalls,
               most keenly, how the stuffy interior grew
                    hotter and hotter
          as they fell through the lower atmosphere
                              lavishly burning down earthward.
     Actual flames shot forth, intermittently,
                    as from a disabled aircraft engine. *Then it was,*
               we grew fearful. We prayed

               to God to let us be not incinerated,
burned alive to charred bone and bubbly ash; and we prayed
          to shuttle the safe trip home.
                    For most of the short time they spent
aboard Sky Lab, they jabbered to each other about lush details
                    of vivid earth scenes below
in their musical native tongue,
          linguistic melting pot
                    of five or six modern languages. Yes, they exulted

                              in the joys of riding the *unmanned*
satellite in the luscious twang of Papiemento,
               their burbly rich accents adorning
               this champagne of verbal wines . . . But all at once,
                    overnight radio monitors
     at NASA, in some anyhowtown Texas, went

into panic!
Someone was transmitting voice signals
in this exotic—though vaguely
familiar—tongue
from within the mute space vehicle itself.
How could this be,
unless Sky Lab had already been hijacked
by aliens or terrorists? But no,
the satellite was continuing to circle
the planet, its course as yet unimpeded, free
and clear. A security whiz

at NASA plugged those ghost voices
into the phone intercom of translators-in-a-multitude-of-
languages, and very quickly,
the spoken tongue of these two glib
chatterboxes (both men: one middle-aged, the other ninety years old
or more, but hardy & clear-
headed), as revealed
by computerized voice prints,
came up Papiemento: no question, a polyglot

language spoken, stylishly,
in the southern Dutch West Indies and a few
of those remotest provinces
in Caribbean towny Venezuela. Thus, promptly,
NASA locating some
expat Arubans living in South Florida,
connected them
by phone to the radio unit in Sky Lab's
cockpit. The Dutchmen, taking
an elitist tack,
recoiled: why had *they* been wakened in the God-
forsaken wee hours
to muddle through staticky exchanges
with mere backwoods Bonaireans,
the wilderness Nature-Park Islanders'
accent spotted at once; and our just-*naturalized*
United States citizen

Arubans could not begin to resist
the urge to pull rank on denizens of their sister island,
        which hadn't yet struck out
            for independence from bullying
Holland. Soon, the four Dutchmen merged in a richly comic banter
                and joking session, much laden
with myth and folklore
        of both isles, the NASA chiefs
            unable to squeeze a word in edgewise, who phoned

                    the Chief Minister of Bonaire
demanding an explanation. The head of state
            had no clue about the suspected
                Sky Lab hijacking . . . Now Pa Francesco and Franz,
                undeterred, reported back
        to their Papiemento mates that Sky Lab's
            precious Black Box
    had just been released, and was dropping
                        toward Bonaire's desert, while our two
                    satellite outlaws
            buzzed to homeland in the next breath. Soon after,
                a team of scouts—
        sent out by the isle's police commissioner
                at the behest of NASA's chief—
departed in a three jeep caravan to hunt
            the fallen computer brain. And recovered intact,
            with no detectable loss

    of its memory bank, the Black Box
was picked up at exactly the desert coordinates relayed
        in Papiemento by a voice
            issuing from the cockpit interior,
just moments before the steely receptacle was expelled and chuted
                safely to earth—its final
lodgment in the Bonaire
        desert, as foretold a week before
            by Pa Francesco. Had he forced the expulsion

of the Black Box from within,
by tripping an eject switch on the controls
panel inside the craft? Perhaps
so, but he'd foreseen the descent and landing
in his clairvoyant vision,
as well. And the satellite's residual shell
fell to earth,
hours later, in southwestern Australia,
also bearing out Pa's prophecy . . .
Many top brass
at NASA, joined by U.S. State Department
emissaries, flew
to Bonaire to look into *bogus charges*
of mystical foul play and hocus
pocus; but touching down on a mere flyspeck
island, they quickly settled for the speediest
return of Sky Lab's jewels.

Romp of the Cave Healer

                                    Of late, I've been death
                        haunted—morbid thoughts sapping my energies,
                                    or nipping my best happy
                        visions in the bud,
                                    each dawn. By midday,
                        I'll have sunk into a quagmire of bitter self muck . . .
                                    Dear Franz leads me
                                    to the dank cave
                        of Pa Malblanco, the monkish shaman healer:
                                    audacious healing bouts held
                                    at infrequent
                                            time sets, Pa never cures

fewer than three or more than seven afflicted souls at a Cave
            Heal-in . . . Four others
      are to be exorcised and rehabbed in my mixed troop
            of gloomsters, sociopaths, and crazies.
      The district judge, after convicting two youths of *domestic mishaps*
            (a young woman
      who stabbed her father, the tailor, with his scissors;
            a precocious teenage boy
                  who'd tried,
            repeatedly, to rape both
      his mom and two younger sisters, succeeded but once
            with the youngest:
preteen nine-year-old), agreed to grant our healing chief shaman
      three sessions to purge the wrongdoers
of the least impulse to commit family malfeasance.
            If Pa Malblanco's
treatments work, if his rebirthing stratagems *take,* those accused

of base felony crimes
shall be given lengthy paroles, their jail
sentences waived. The last two
in our ensemble:
a middle-aged woman,
struck down by grief when her three boys were zapped
by a fire that swept
through their house
one night—she hurtled from the second story,
smallest son blanket-wrapped
and cradled
in her arms (already snuffed

by smoke inhalation); she broke both legs, convinced she'd kept
her Alfred alive,
chary to relinquish her grip on the shredding blanket
for days thereafter, two men having to wrestle
a child cadaver from her bed before the stench drew rats & mongrels—
in a few more hours,
they'd have fought off *those varmints*. Now she wanders
the desert nights imploring
her lost sons
to return home, or she chants
wild monologues to ghosts of her long-dead father
and grandmother . . .
Who's left? A routine schizophrenic housewife. Of late, she shits
in the laundry tub and, nightly, beds down
with her old dray horse in the stable. *How do I fit in,*
mute tagalong
with this bleak gallery of the crestfallen? . . . We enter the cave

single file, each wound
in a rope chain taken twice about our waists
like mountain climber's gear.
If one of us
should misstep or fall
in cave dark, the next in line shall rescue the stumbler
(or drag him, helpless,
limbs flopping

           on the cave bottom rocks: small comfort there) . . .
                    I ponder my place in the *buddy*
               chain, wedged between
                         patricide and a sister

rapist; I had better see to my own flatfooted, halting gait.
        No flashlights permitted,
    but our guru carries a single low candle, its light
        guttering down in the dish. The little pool
of wax threatens to douse the short wick, sputtery. Our shadows,
        thrown on the cave top
    as we walk, loom wider and taller with every step.
        At first, we duck our heads to keep
             from scraping
    our scalps on the roof, or low-
hanging stalactites. Soon the ceiling loft expands
        higher and higher
becoming, at last, a capacious amphitheater that has been gouged
    and hacked from the great walls of coral.
We continue our journey, in lock step, for a half mile
    or more, our shadows
grown to gigantic hulks above . . . Pa Malblanco grunts an abrupt

                         halt, quenches the candle.
        Two bluish lights sweep from wall to wall
                    overhead, we hear bats flutter
             and swish: do bat wings
                 irradiate the blue flash,
        aglimmer like fireflies' luminous abdomens? Blue gleams
             surge and dim and surge,
                 circling the roof
        dome of the high arena we all now inhabit.
             Malblanco bids us to squat,
             and we sit cross-
                 legged, our open hands

cupped over our knees, eyes fixed upon the concave arch above,
        as in an Astrodome
    or planetarium. And indeed, those intense blue lights—

stationary now—could be planets or stars.
Our mentor climbs a squarish flat-topped rock. Seated in a circle
   around this instant
stage set, we can just make out his bowed silhouette,
   arms swinging from side to side
      before him
   like an orangutan's. Then he stands
and rocks forward on the balls of his bare feet.
   His breath comes scratchy,
he groans and sweeps his hands up and down and across his belly
   massaging his innards, and at last, he makes
gurgles and great squishing sounds as if he, himself, is
   a fetus struggling
to burst from its mother's womb. Now he lies on his side, and starts

                              rolling counterclockwise
         on the flat mossy rock like a human top
                    spinning faster and faster.
         Those gurgle sounds
            grow louder and slurpier,
      and finally, we hear a great rush of waters pour from him.
         Soon we are all spattered
            with a fine spray.
      I lick a few drops from the back of my hand.
         It tastes pure as spring water
            that I sampled
               earlier today; and yes,

he's tossing water on us with a long wooden ladle, scoopings
      drawn from a secret well
   below his legs. It tastes wonderful, rich and clean.
      And then he leaps in a birthing dance, plays
   the child newborn, howling its first breath wails of life & spewing
      out amniotic waters—
         foam gushed from the ruptured birth sac over our faces
         and into our eyes. We stare down
            that plethora
         of bubbles and spray, now a froth

on our lips, and we commence howling with our master.
    We have all risen
to our feet at once, unbidden, and leap as he leaps, those ropes
    still binding our waists. So we must jump
in unison, five hopscotch leapers on the springboards
    of our rope-jump souls,
hopping in place in perfect sync and simpatico with each other,

                the ropes flying loose
    with our romp. Though no one signals another
        to keep in step, we can all hear
    the inaudible beat,
        and we know this dance.
We first heard the rhythm the day we were born. Hours before
    we were born, the cycle
    of labor pangs—
coming in waves—gave us this motion, never
    forgotten, revived this day.
    Likewise, we know
    the timbre of Pa's howls.

We first sang them at our first births. And today, they sing
    themselves again, using
our throats in chorus, no two of our five voices
    ever drifting out of perfect accord.
And more amazing yet, it does not surprise us for even a moment
    that we should all rise
to the same pitch, stomp and chant to the same beat,
    and know—all together—when it
    shall be time
to stop . . . The starry blue lights,
    fixed in place as we wailed and leapt, start wheeling
    and circling overhead,
fluttery, whooshing as bat wings. Now Pa waves his candle, relit
    in its shallow dish, and leads us back
the way we came, those guide ropes no longer needed.
    We emerge from the cave
mouth, a family of five, laughing and weeping our blustery thanks.

Compass of the Dying

That hoop-back man,
　　in wide brim straw hat,
　　　　clomps past on a donkey. Franz calls
　　　　a halt: Pa Guillermo
revolves on his bareback mule perch to greet us.
Himself a first generation son of slaves, now in his mid-
　　　　　　eighties, Guillermo's voice
　　　　　　rumbles and hisses like a rusty antique
　　Ford radiator
　　　　boiling over. His voice waves—
　　　　　　in presence of witnesses—have blown
　　　　　　that three ton volcanic rock across the grassy
flat-topped mesa . . .

　　　　　　　　He *sounds out* family earth plots
　　　　　　　　with divining rods,
　　　　　　his guttural hum snorting as he measures and sighs
　　　　　　　　　　and inches his way
　　　　toward the best place, the perfect
　　　　　　　　site, to build a house. Tapping the ground, his touch

shivers: he traces
　　minute pulls, or infinites-
　　　　imal repulsings; he feels their sucks,
　　　　or rebuffs, on the pads
of bare toes. *Magnets underground,* he lovingly names
that occult force: tap, tap—he listens for echoes, and fathoms
　　　　　　the hidden palpitant life
　　　　　　of terrestrial currents. And when he knows,
　　he knows in gulfs
　　　　of his bone marrow. *Build here.*
　　　　　　Lay the cornerstone there, not yonder.

Make your house foundations radiate to northwest,
not southeast; yessir,

              there can be no mistake about it . . .
                  And long-lived
     though he be, his health on an even keel, he knows
                 the secrets of dying.
   They rush him to bedside vigils
        to chant and hum and teach the breather of last breaths

how to expire.
     And if time permits,
         Guillermo leads him to the right place
        to lay his head. Where
to die, how to embrace death—he is the best guide
for dying. More and more, he says, he turns to the animals
           for answers to those last
          questions. He shepherds us afoot, yet never
    leaving his donkey
      roost, to a secret place
        beside high pileup of lava boulders,
        a perennial graveyard of the animals. He pokes
with his gnarled stick,

         pushes aside a weedy furze patch
           loosely braided
     over a shallow pit: brimful of rain-polished bones,
           bones of all shapes
   and sizes—no solitary animal
       species claims this dying zone. All land-rover denizens

of Bonaire—*save men*—
    though natural enemies
       they may be in life, share this common
      grave site. If we pick
through the bone pile, we find the brittle vertebrae
of lizard, iguana, nestled beside goat skull, donkey leg bone,
       sheep hip shank, wild turkey

or duck breastbones—which bespeak a commonalty
in the dying
breaths . . . The animals gather,
punctually, often three or four in tandem,
at the death pits. They may wander miles, or a mere
one hundred meters,

perhaps, to the nearest mass grave.
Consult Guillermo,
at any hour, at any far reach of this small country's
outsweep: he'll escort you,
forthwith, to the closest death plot.
There are many such, scattered about the cunucu desert.

He finds them, always,
with unerring surety
of gauge—as if some internal death
compass pointed its dial.
Does scent of the dying carcass linger in the air,
long after the flesh has rotted away, the bones scoured clean?
How do those animals,
shambling and dragging crushed limbs, near-lame
with fatal wounds
and gasping last breaths, find
their way? *The hidden magnets draw them,*
he intones. *It's nothing you can hear or see or smell,*
no senses touch it,

our instruments can't measure it,
but earth's pull
on the dying beast is great—he can't resist its tugs.
I, too, feel pulsings
below, though I'm not ailing yet.
The animals know pain, pain—O how they are hurting! Here

come they, when death
throes be upon them, to die
quicker, they come to die more easily,

to welcome the last stirrings
of life and greet death's snaggle-toothed clean bite . . .
So it is, great heaps of bones collect there. Pa Guillermo, still
        propped on his mule, now circles
          the volcanic rock pile and stops at a dung heap,
    where the layers
       upon layers of poop beyond
         reckoning have been strewn by a wide range
        of sick or bruised creatures, fresh manures splashed,
daily, into the ever-

         dank and fetid compost. Hereupon,
            the wounded beasts,
     not dying, not dying, come to heal themselves, and here
             they find rich poultice
or succor for their hurts, whereby
       they recover their strength, and revive their lost powers.

The healing grounds,
    like those mass grave sites,
       are scattered, randomly, over the desert.
       Survivors, of whatever species,
may crawl, limp, creep, or shuffle to the nearest. *And how*
do the hurt animals know, I ask, *if it's a time to die, or a time*
        to be healed? . . . They're not humans,
       he replies. *It is never in doubt. They* must *know!*
    It is one time
     or the other. Confusion, doubt,
       that is our *invention. Always, a hurt critter*
       knows which time it is—whether time to finish, or time
to begin again.

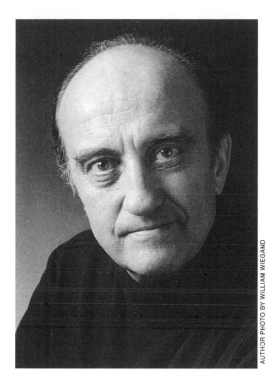

LAURENCE LIEBERMAN has published ten
books of poetry. His work has appeared in
Best American Poetry and has been widely
anthologized. "Lament for the Lady Felons"
from this collection appeared in *The World's
Best Poetry.* He has received grants from the
National Endowment for the Arts and
fellowships from Yaddo and the Huntington
Hartford Foundation. He taught English
and did research for many years in the
Virgin Islands and across the Caribbean and
is currently professor of English at the
University of Illinois, Champaign-Urbana.